THE SHEFFIELD STAR
RAILWAY ALBUM

Compiled by Clive Hardy

★ The Star

at heart ♡ publications

First published in 2008 by
At Heart Ltd
32 Stamford Street
Altrincham
Cheshire
WA14 1EY

in conjunction with
The Sheffield Star
York Street
Sheffield
Yorkshire
S1 1PU

ISBN: 978-1-84547-206-1

Printed and bound by Ashford Colour Press, Gosport.

Both Sheffield Midland and Sheffield Victoria were something of a Mecca for boys of all ages armed with notebooks for taking down engine numbers, perhaps an Ian Allan shed book to see where particular engines came from. Ian Allan also produced a series of regional books.

INTRODUCTION

Welcome to *The Sheffield Star Railway Album*, a combined selection of picture library and readers' images from the 19th to the 21st centuries. First and foremost, this is not an illustrated railway history of the Sheffield area, though we hope the content will be of interest to general reader and enthusiast alike. The book is divided into sections, a couple of which – 'Along Midland Lines' and 'Along Great Central Lines' – are laid out geographically as well as chronologically, though we did have problems dating several images as they carried publication dates rather than dates taken. In the world of evening newspapers that can mean a difference of 20 or 30 years, as a popular image will appear over and over again.

'Along Great Central Lines' kicks off at Dinting with a look round the Dinting Railway Centre, then takes us to the scene of the derailment of a Barton–Immingham anhydrous ammonia tank train at Hadfield on 8 April 1981. Then it's off via Torside, Crowden and Woodhead to Penistone, Wortley and Sheffield Victoria.

'Send it by Rail' takes a look at freight traffic and handling, as well as the hustle and bustle that once accompanied a train's arrival, as staff loaded and unloaded parcels and post. We also join *Star* reporter Martin Dawes to see what happens to a letter he posted on a night mail train from Sheffield Midland. This section also includes pictures of the fire at the Wicker goods depot.

'On Shed' features a number of pictures taken at Millhouses, Grimesthorpe, Darnall engine sheds and Tinsley Traction Maintenance Depot. It also includes images of locomotives with a Sheffield connection taken elsewhere.

'Rotherham, Barnsley, Swinton and Doncaster' covers a wide number of topics: from floods at Rotherham in the 1930s to the opening of the new station at Swinton, bomb disposal at Barnsley Station to the 'Farewell to the Deltics' day at Doncaster Works.

The final section is on the Sheffield Supertram. Why cover this in a railway book? Well, the Supertram has more in common with a light railway than the City of Sheffield street trams of old. Supertrams stop at stations rather than tramstops, they are controlled by a sophisticated signalling system that is integrated with road traffic light sequencing, and the whole setup comes under the jurisdiction of the Railways Inspectorate.

Stanier Jubilee Class 4-6-0 5XP No.45598 *Basutoland* at Sheffield Midland on 10 June 1964. (C.M. & J.M. Bentley)

Here are a few tips for readers with little or no railway knowledge. Steam locomotives are often referred to by the surname of the Chief Mechanical Engineer responsible for their overall concept, the class they belong to, power output and wheel arrangement. It's not as difficult as it sounds. The picture (left) features Stanier Jubilee Class 5XP 4-6-0 No.45598 *Basutoland* at Sheffield Midland. In other words, the engine was designed by Sir William Stanier of the London Midland & Scottish Railway (LMS). The LMS Board designated these engines the Jubilee Class, as the first of them appeared around the time of the Silver Jubilee of King George V and Queen Mary. The 5XP is simply the engine's power output as an express engine. A 4P would be less powerful, a 6P more. *Basutoland* is a 4-6-0 meaning it is equipped with a four-wheel leading bogie and six driving wheels; the wheels under the tender do not count. A 0-6-0T has six coupled wheels and no tender. Its coal is carried in a bunker behind the cab and its water in tanks either side of the boiler. A 0-6-0ST is similar, except the water is carried in a tank that straddles the top of the boiler a bit like a saddle on a horse.

Diesel classifications change in the late 1960s with the introduction of computer records (TOPS). When the system was first went live, the higher the class number was, the more powerful the locomotive. So Class 01 were shunting engines of less than 200hp, whilst Class 55 were the famous 3000hp Napier Deltics of the East Coast Main Line. All electric locomotives and railcars are allocated a class number, and steam engines cleared to run over Network Rail can also be identified through the TOPS system. Main line diesel and electric locomotives each have two powered bogies. A Bo-Bo has two bogies each with two powered axles; a Co-Co has two bogies each with three powered axles; a 1Co-Co1 has two bogies each with an unpowered axle at the leading end.

A quick word about Up and Down. All railway running lines are either Up or Down and there are lots of different ones such as Up Slow, Down Fast, Up & Down Fast and so on. Historically the terms came about to identify the direction of travel, and in the 19th century, Up lines were always in the direction of the most important town on the route. So a train from Derby to London would travel on the Up line whilst a train from London to Derby would travel on the Down line.

Now the main thing to do is sit back and enjoy the sights, if not the sounds, echoing from these pages. For those of you who wish to find out more about railways around Sheffield there are some excellent books published by Foxline, Oakwood Press, OPC and Ian Allan.

Clive Hardy

ALONG MIDLAND LINES

Stanier Jubilee 5XP 4-6-0 No.45597 heads north out of Chesterfield. On the right is Chesterfield Wagon Works. (C.M. & J.M. Bentley)

Stanier 8F 2-8-0 No.48271 trundles through Tapton Junction at the head of a mixed freight. (C.M. & J.M. Bentley)

Line closures for heavy engineering works used to happen in BR days, though not with the frequency imposed by either Network Rail or its predecessor, Railtrack. This picture, taken by photographer David Vaughan in August 1969 for publication in the *Morning Telegraph*, shows engineers putting the finishing touches to their preparations to blow the 'lid' off Broomhouse Tunnel on the Sheffield–Chesterfield line.

The line was closed to all traffic on 17 August, the tunnel roof being demolished with explosives two days later. The line reopened to traffic on 7 September with trains being diverted during the intervening weeks. The diversion routes were via Barrow Hill, Beighton Junction, and Rotherham Masbro' for north-bound passenger trains, while freight went via Kirkby and Mansfield.

Broomhouse Tunnel, or rather Broomhouse Cutting, is open for business again. Interestingly the tunnel length on the old Midland Railway route maps was always shown as 92 yards, yet here the old tunnel sign states 88 yards.

Dronfield closed to passengers on 2 September 1967 and by the time *The Star* reported, in July 1979, that it would be reopening, there was little left of this once attractive station. On 8 October 1980, members of Derbyshire County Council and the North East Derbyshire & District Council visited the station to see how work was progressing on rehabilitating the site. When the station finally reopened on 5 January 1981 it seemed as though the whole town had turned out to watch the first train leave for Sheffield.

During 2008, the 2027-yard-long Bradway Tunnel between Dronfield and Dore & Totley South Junction is to be closed to traffic for relining, as well as track and drainage works. The blockage will last three months and will cost many hundreds of thousands of pounds. In January 1964 one of our photographers was given access to repair work then being carried out. For years, the tunnel had suffered the effects of water damage and part of the brick lining had bulged out of alignment.

During the 1990s the problem once again became acute and Railtrack undertook major repairs as part of the upgrading of the Midland Main Line network. This involved replacing the bulged brickwork, but before this could be undertaken the integrity of the tunnel lining had to secured. Specialists Weldgrip Geotechnic were called in by the main contractors. They used their high-density rockbolts and a polymer geogrid to create a support system so that the bulged area could be cut away and replaced.

A new use for the station building at Dore. The sign reads F.S. Rastall (Printers) Ltd.

Stanier Jubilee Class 4-6-0 No.45651 *Shovell* rattles through Dore & Totley Station at the head of a south-bound express. The track layout was altered here during 1901, when Up and Down slow lines as far as Heeley Carriage Sidings were laid. The picture dates from 1960. (C.M. & J.M. Bentley)

Once known as Abbey House, Beauchief Station was sandwiched between Dore & Totley and Millhouses & Ecclesall. It closed to passengers on 2 January 1961 and to goods traffic on 15 June 1964. During its lifetime the station had several names. It opened as Abbey House but was officially renamed Beauchief on 1 April 1870. By May 1874 it was called Beauchieff (note the double 'f') & Abbey Dale, losing the second 'f' in December 1889. It was renamed Beauchief on 9 March 1914.

The overgrown platforms of Millhouses & Ecclesall Station on 25 July 1975.

By the early 1860s Sheffield was still without a direct rail route to the south via Chesterfield, though by 1863 the Midland had come up with some rough plans and had agreed that the old Sheffield & Rotherham Station at Wicker would be replaced by a new large station situated off Pond Street.

Work began once Parliamentary powers for the new line had been obtained; preliminary work included the compulsory purchase and subsequent demolition of over 1000 houses along the southern approaches to Sheffield. Construction was relatively slow, due in part to some unexpected civil engineering, and eventually opened for traffic on 1 February 1870. On that day Wicker closed to passenger traffic and services were transferred to Sheffield New Midland Station though for some reason without any official ceremony.

Our picture shows the canopied entrance to the new station, which was accessed by way of a drive from Pond Street. The building included separate booking offices for different classes of traveller, first and second class ladies' and gentlemen's waiting rooms and two classes of refreshment rooms.

During the early 1900s, the Midland spent over £215,000 upgrading the station. The building pictured here survived, although it now houses station facilities on what are now island platforms 2-5. A new enlarged entrance with a 300ft covered way was added, as was a new platform 1.

Having arrived at St Pancras, members of Sheffield Wednesday's 1935 FA Cup Final side pose for the cameraman. Seated from left to right are: Mark Hooper, Ronnie Starling, Ted Catlin and Jack Brown.

No.600 was one of a batch of Class 2P inside-cylinder 4-4-0 light passenger engines built at Derby in 1928, and is pictured here at Sheffield Midland on 4 May 1929. A close look shows that when they were built, these engines also had brakes on their bogie, a feature later removed by William Stanier. (W.L. Good courtesy Gordon Coltas Photographic Trust)

2P 4-4-0 No. 383 was one of the original Midland Railway engines and ended its days allocated to Derby, where it was withdrawn from service in July 1952. This picture was taken on 4 May 1929. (W.L. Good courtesy Gordon Coltas Photographic Trust)

Grimesthorpe-based mixed traffic 'Crab' 2-6-0 No.13097 pictured at Sheffield Midland on 4 May 1929. The concept for these engines originated with the Caledonian Railway prior to the Grouping in 1923. LMS Chief Mechanical Engineer George Hughes reworked the design several times so that the engines would fit within the English loading gauge, hence the rakish incline of the cylinders and the high running plate.

Hughes retired before construction of the first engine No.13000 began at Horwich Works, and his successor Henry Fowler insisted on a number of changes such as the use of the standard 3500 gallon tender. The first 100 were finished in Crimson Lake passenger livery and the class as a whole proved efficient and reliable.

The nickname 'Crab' is said to have come about because of their ungainly pincer-like cylinder and valve gear layout. (C.M. & J.M. Bentley)

Soon to be disappearing from a station buffet near you? The ubiquitous British Railways sandwich: the butt of many a joke, and since the Tory privatisation of the 1990s, one of the few bad things people have to say about the former nationalised railway.

This picture possibly dates from October 1939, as during the following month the railway sarnie became one of the first victims of wartime rationing. People were obviously enjoying them too much! Despite millions being sold every year, it was announced that the sandwiches would soon be disappearing from refreshment rooms across the nation. Passengers were told not to worry, however, as there would soon be a replacement in the shape of a wartime standard British Railways beef sandwich but, perhaps thankfully, it never happened.

Looking resplendent, even in wartime unlined black livery, LMS Coronation Class Pacific No.6249 *City of Sheffield* simmers gently at Sheffield Midland on 1 November 1944 during her official naming ceremony. (D. Ibbotson)

A nameplate from *City of Sheffield* is presented to the Lord Mayor Alderman J.S. Worrall and the Corporation in July 1963.

British Railway's uniforms altered little from what they had been under the LMS, LNER, GWR and SR. In 1963, new styles began to be trialled and the Press had a field day when the final selection was made. The main criticism of the new uniforms were the caps, which most of the Press reported as looking as though they had been borrowed from Rommel's Afrika Corps. Our Pictures show the BR uniform as worn by staff at Sheffield Midland in the 1950s and the new design under trial in Scotland in 1963.

Train spotters while away the day.

A Royal Scot Class 4-6-0 No.46109 *Royal Engineer* waits the road. The Royal Scots came about almost by accident. At the Grouping, the West Coast Anglo-Scottish expresses were hauled by former LNWR Claughton Class four-cylinder 4-6-0s. Though fast, they were heavy on coal and even heavier on repair costs, despite a series of modifications carried out by the LMS.

Had things turned out the way Sir Henry Fowler wanted, the Claughtons would have been replaced by a class of four-cylinder compound 4-6-0s built to a reworked design first suggested by George Hughes. As it was, the LMS managed to borrow a new Castle Class 4-6-0 off the GWR and trialled it on expresses between Euston and Crewe and later Carlisle. The Castle proved a winner, so much so that the LMS Board are said to have wanted to place an immediate order for 50 of them, but reconsidered only when it was pointed out that there would be loading gauge problems.

Desperate to have new engines in service in time for the 1927 summer timetable, the LMS turned to the North British Locomotive Co of Glasgow who pulled out all the stops both on the design as well as the building. The initial order for 50 was split between North British's Hyde Park and Queen's Road plants, delivering No.6100 to the LMS on 14 July about five months after the order was officially placed. The last engine was delivered on 15 November. So successful were these engines that a further 20 were built at Derby Works and delivered during May 1930.

A trio of 4-4-0 Class 4P express passenger 'crimson ramblers' at Sheffield Midland during the 1950s. Based on a former Midland Railway design, a total of 195 of these three-cylinder compounds were built for the LMS between 1924 and 1932. On the right is No.41191 which was allocated to Millhouses shed in June 1952. It was transferred to Leeds in September 1955, finally being withdrawn in March 1956. The covered trainsheds pictured here were demolished in the autumn of 1956. Damaged during the war, BR considered them beyond economical repair.

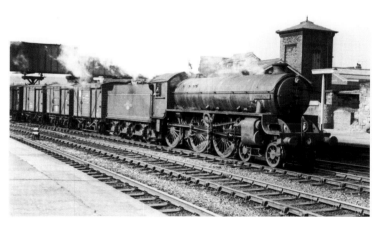

Thompson B1 4-6-0 No.61021 *Reitbok* trundles through Sheffield Midland with a rake of vans on 8 June 1964. Without doubt it was Edward Thompson's most successful design during his five-year reign as Chief Mechanical Engineer of the LNER.

The B1s were the first two-cylinder main line engines built by the LNER as Thompson's predecessor Sir Nigel Gresley was a three-cylinder man. Wartime construction constraints meant that the first ten were not completed until 1944, but once peace was declared, Thompson was able to place orders with the North British Locomotive Co, Glasgow, and Vulcan Foundry, Newton-le-Willows. Construction continued into the BR era, finally ceasing in 1952 by which time the class comprised 410 units. Darnall based B1s were regularly scheduled to haul *The Master Cutler*.

No.61021's unusual name derives from the fact that the completion of the prototype B1, No.8301, coincided with a visit to Great Britain by the Prime Minister of South Africa, General Smuts. Consequently the engine was named *Springbok* in his honour and all 40 B1s received names of breeds of South African antelope. (C.M. & J.M. Bentley)

Bo-Bo Type 2 D5550, seen here at Sheffield Midland in January 1966, was one of a large class of low axle load, high route availability, diesel-electrics built for BR between November 1957 and November 1962 by Brush Traction of Loughborough.

The first 20 of these locomotives were ordered under the BR Pilot Scheme, the aim of which was to evaluate a number of designs from BR itself as well as from commercial locomotive manufacturers prior to ordering production runs. These particular locos were technically similar to 25 diesel-electrics built by Brush for Ceylon in 1950. They had the same AIA-AIA wheel arrangement and Mirrlees JVS12T power plant; however, the BR locos were heavier at 104 tons against 87 tons, and had a redesigned cab. D5500 was completed during September 1959 and made its trial run to Chinley on 10 October.

Not all the new diesels proved successful. Among the turkeys were ten 800hp Type 1 Bo-Bos built by the North British Locomotive Co between May and September 1958. That D8400–D8409 were underpowered and unable to work in multiple with other classes of diesels were the least of their problems, and the lot were condemned in 1968.

The preserved Gresley A3 Pacific *Flying Scotsman* eases through Sheffield Midland on 7 May 1969. The engine, complete with two tenders to increase its range between stops for water, was en route to pick up the Eisenhower coaches for Liverpool.

Iconic steam locomotive *Flying Scotsman* put in an appearance at Sheffield Midland on 25 September 1973. On the footplate driver Jim Godber (left) of Tinsley Depot explains the workings to the Master Cutler, Mr Richard Doncaster.

Over the years *Flying Scotsman* has paid a number of visits to Sheffield. Here she is again entering Sheffield in June 1980.

Preserved LNER three-cylinder Class V2 2-6-2 No 4771 *Green Arrow* heads a special out of Sheffield Midland on 21 September 1975. In the same year, it took part in the Rail 150 cavalcade at Shildon, celebrating the 150th anniversary of the opening of the Stockton & Darlington Railway. No.4771 was withdrawn from service in 1987 and did not venture out again until August 1998, following a two-year overhaul which was in fact the first in-house restoration to be undertaken by the National Railway Museum.

From May 2007, the V2 was relegated to making appearances on heritage lines after a boiler inspection had revealed heavy wear to the firebox foundation rings. This was in additional to the crack in its unique monobloc cylinder casting. On 1 April 2008 the NRM ordered *Green Arrow* – which was on a visit to the North Yorkshire Moors Railway – to be withdrawn from service following the discovery of cracked superheater flues. However the NYMR engineers were able to carry out temporary repairs, allowing the V2 to make one last run prior to its ticket expiring.

Stanier Princess Coronation Class 8P 4-6-2 No.46229 *Duchess of Hamilton* at Sheffield. Like the LNER's Gresley A4s, the LMS Princess Coronations were streamlined; even Nos.6235 to 6248 which were built during the war. However, the streamline casing was removed from all of the class between 1945 and 1949. As well as *Duchess of Hamilton*, No.6233 *Duchess of Sutherland* and No.46235 *City of Birmingham* are also preserved.

Between 2007 and 2008 the Tyseley Locomotive Works work began refitting a streamlined casing to *Duchess of Hamilton*, but ran into a problem sourcing the correct 3000mm by 2000mm by 1.5mm thick sheeting. The only steelworks at present able to produce sheeting to this specification is in China, and this only in quantities of 1000 tonnes.

Sheffield's £2 million power signalbox was commissioned during the weekend of 20–22 January 1973, and in doing so replaced boxes Sheffield A and B, Sheffield Nos.1 and 2, Heeley Station, Heeley carriage sidings, Millhouses, and Queen's Road. Temporary panel boxes remained operational at Dore & Totley and Brightside.

The Lord Mayor of Sheffield, Alderman S. Kenneth Arnold, is given a tour of the relay room at the new power signalbox at Sheffield Midland. Explaining the system is divisional signal and telecommunications engineer W.G. Boddy (right). On the left by the pillar is J.B. Peile, a member of the BR (Eastern) Board.

Built on the site of Pond Street goods depot, Sheaf House, BR's new headquarters building for the Sheffield Division allowed previously dispersed departments to be brought together under one roof. Among the locations declared redundant were the former Duke of Norfolk's house just east of the Chesterfield lines, and the Control Offices at Victoria and Rotherham Westgate.

On 11 May 1973 BR invited the Master Cutler, Mr Richard Doncaster, to have a look round the Class 47 Co-Co diesel-electric locomotive hauling *The Master Cutler*. Pictured with the Master and Mistress Cutler are Mr G. Myers, Divisional Manager of British Rail and stationmaster Mr R. Tunnicliffe.

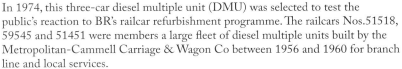

In 1974, this three-car diesel multiple unit (DMU) was selected to test the public's reaction to BR's railcar refurbishment programme. The railcars Nos.51518, 59545 and 51451 were members a large fleet of diesel multiple units built by the Metropolitan-Cammell Carriage & Wagon Co between 1956 and 1960 for branch line and local services.

As well as completely refurbished interiors, the unit was finished in a new livery of off-white with a blue waistband. In fact, at the time this picture was taken the livery on the opposite side differed slightly in that the blue band was deeper. The unit also sports the South Yorkshire Passenger Transport Executive (PTE) logo, to be carried by trains allocated to Linkline local services. This set was sent on a tour of PTEs sporting the requisite logo at each one.

A taste of things to come for passengers taking advantage of the revamped Trans-Pennine timetable in May 1979. This Class 123 DMU, with accommodation equivalent to that found in locomotive-hauled coaches, was on display at Sheffield Midland. However, these Leyland Albion-engined units weren't new. They had in fact been built at Swindon in 1963 for use on the Swansea–Birmingham–Derby InterCity services, but ended up leading a somewhat nomadic existence. They were first used on Cardiff–Bristol–Portsmouth trains, followed by a move to Reading to work to Paddington–Oxford route, before moving back to Cardiff to work Cardiff–Crewe services.

During the late 1970s the 123s were transferred to Botanic Gardens, Hull, on the Eastern Region. Botanic Gardens had recently been re-equipped as a maintenance depot for units fitted with Leyland Albion engines which had also resulted in the purpose-built Class 124 'Trans-Pennine' units being transferred there from Leeds Neville Hill depot. That both classes had the same power units enabled BR to operate sets in mix-and-match formations. All were withdrawn by summer 1984 and replaced by locomotive-hauled trains.

British Rail's second generation DMU building programme was launched in 1981 when Derby Litchurch Lane Works completed the prototype two-car railbus No.14001, comprising cars 55500 and 55501. Apart from the driving cabs, they were little more than a couple of Leyland National bus bodies mounted on four-wheeled underframes; even the 102 seats were bus type. There was a gangway connection between the two vehicles and No.55501 also had a lavatory.

Four classes of railbuses were built during the 1980s. The first, the Class 141s, were direct descendants of No.14001 and were built at Derby in 1984. These were followed in 1985-86 by 96 two-car Class 142s which were slightly wider and better looking, and they in turn were followed by the Class 143s which had body shells from coach builders W. Alexander, and frames designed by commercial locomotive manufacturers Andrew Barclay & Co. The final class, the 144s, were again by Alexander, but this time British Rail Engineering Ltd supplied the underframes. Some 143s and 144s were fitted with Voith T2IIr hydraulic transmission.

Another prototype to visit Sheffield Midland was the three-car Class 150 diesel multiple unit No.15001. Built at York, production classes comprised the 150/1 and 150/2s. These were two-car sets the main difference between them being that the 150/2s were gangwayed throughout, enabling two or more sets to be worked together as one train by one crew.

The highly successful 2500hp 1Co-Co1 Sulzer Type 4 diesel-electrics Nos. D1–D183 entered service between 1959 and 1963 and for nearly two decades dominated London Midland passenger workings out of St Pancras. In February 1960, D13 was used on trials to access the type's freight handling capabilities on the Woodhouse Junction to Ulceby (Lincs) section of the Sheffield–Retford–Grimsby route.

Leading attendant Fred Howarth (left) and Attendant Michael Wood (right) lay the tables in the First Class dining car on an InterCity service for Sheffield.

In 1983, ten InterCity 125 sets were transferred from the Great Western to the former Midland line out of St Pancras to work Sheffield–Nottingham–Derby services. The first HST 125s went into service on the Western Region in October 1976; each set consisting of seven passenger cars and two power cars. Sets for the East Coast Main Line had an additional passenger car.

A track gang takes advantage of the January 1982
strike to get on with a little maintenance work.

From January 1984 travellers at Sheffield Midland were able to
obtain up to the minute information on trains via TV monitors
positioned at various locations around the station.

Preserved Stanier Black Five 4-6-0 No.5305 pulls away from Sheffield Midland with the Thames & Eden Pullman tour in March 1983. Steam traction on scheduled BR services ended on 3 August 1968, the final workings being the 2050hrs Preston–Blackpool and the 2125hrs Preston–Liverpool Exchange. Afterwards there were a number of specials, including one organised by BR themselves: a Manchester Victoria to Southport and back behind No.45305.

Preserved LNER A4 pacific No.4498 *Sir Nigel Gresley* steams into Sheffield at the head of The White Rose rail tour in February 1988. On 2 July 1988 this locomotive, along with two other surviving A4s, were paraded at the National Railway Museum, York, as part of celebrations marking the 50th anniversary of *Mallard* capturing the world speed record for steam traction. One of these was *Mallard* itself, the other was 60019 *Bittern* cunningly disguised as LNER No.2509 *Silver Link* complete with side valancing and specially repainted in the stunning blue and grey livery carried by the first four A4s. The following day, BR's latest electric locomotive No.89001 hauled its first booked passenger service – the Mallard 50th anniversary special –

from Kings Cross to Doncaster. From there *Mallard* herself took over for a run to Scarborough and back. On 10 August No.89001 was again in the news, this time hauling the first electric passenger service between London and Leeds: the 0820hrs from Kings Cross. The return working departed Leeds at 1200hrs.

It is May 1990 and *Flying Scotsman* once again draws the crowds to Sheffield Midland. The headboard proudly displays the fact that during her 27-day tour of Australia, *Flying Scotsman* covered 4000 miles.

Another unique steam locomotive putting in an appearance in 1990 was the preserved BR Standard Class 8P 4-6-2 No.71000 *Duke of Gloucester*. Out of 999 Standard locomotives built to BR designs, this engine was the only one with three cylinders. It was also the first to have a double chimney and the first to be fitted with British Caprotti valve gear, which resulted in excellent steam distribution. The boiler was identical to that fitted on the BR Britannia Class Pacifics.

No.71000 was a regular performer on the *Mid-day Scot* express which was one of the heaviest passenger trains (around 500 tons) in the country in the 1950s. It ran on the tightest of schedules too, having to cover the 82 miles between Euston and Rugby in 80 minutes.

The engine was withdrawn in November 1962 and stored at Crewe. The left hand cylinder and valve gear were removed for display in the Science Museum, Kensington, and No.71000 was sent to Woodhams Scrapyard, Barry, for cutting up. It was eventually rescued and returned to service.

Sheffield Star photographer Steve Ellis was at Sheffield Midland on 23 February 1994 taking snow pictures when in rolled preserved West Country Class 4-6-2 No.34027 *Taw Valley* with its support coach.

Preserved Princess Royal Class 4-6-2 *Princess Margaret Rose* passes
through Sheffield Midland at the head of a railtour on 18 March 1994.

Rather nice detail from Midland Station with ornate iron and brickwork. Above the entrance is a Wyvern, the mythical creature that appeared on the Midland Railway coat of arms.

British Rail gets in the Christmas mood in December 1970.

Queen Elizabeth II inspects a military guard of honour drawn up from
the Yorkshire Volunteers during her visit to Sheffield on 29 July 1975.

"May the force be with you." British Transport Police Inspector David Mabbott, Sgt Michael Carrington and PC Paul Cullen, prepare to board BR's anti-vandal 'Q' Train at Sheffield Midland. The 'Q' trains patrolled lines where known acts of vandalism had taken place on a regular basis. The train looked like an ordinary passenger train but had authorisation to stop in section should the need arise. The 'Q' comes from the 'Q' ships of World War One. These were merchant vessels equipped with hidden guns, the idea being to entice German U-boats to the surface whereupon the merchant vessel could open fire at close range.

Driver George Keighley takes his turn at the controls of a diesel
multiple unit which has been diagrammed for 'Q' Train duties.

Sergeant
Keith Groves
of the British
Transport Police
rides shotgun
for the driver of
the 'Q' Train.

An artist's impression of the major regeneration scheme planned for Sheffield to include remodelling Sheaf Square, sandblasting the station frontage and the creation of an open pedestrian space with retail outlets. The £35 million project, sponsored by Midland Mainline, also included a new footbridge across the full width of the station, and connecting it with the Supertram station. The tramway itself would be realigned for ease of access by pedestrians.

ALONG GREAT
CENTRAL LINES

Preserved Stanier Jubilee Class 4-6-0s No.5690 *Leander* and No.5596 *Bahamas* were the star turns at the Dinting Railway Centre during this open day held in August 1975.

Visitors to the open day at the Dinting Railway Centre near Glossop on 23 October 1975 were able to experience footplate rides on a 0-4-0ST built by Andrew Barclay & Co of Kilmarnock in 1949.

Inside the exhibition hall at Dinting Railway Centre. Of interest here is the second engine from the left. This is No.1054, the sole survivor of a once 300-strong class of 2F 0-6-2Ts built at Crewe between 1881 and 1897 for the London & North Western Railway (LNWR). Designed by Francis Webb, these relatively reliable engines were known as 'Coal Tanks' not because of their role, but simply because they were a tank engine version of Webb's 0-6-0 Coal Engines.

Sixty-four survived into BR ownership. The last, No.58926 (No.1054) was withdrawn from Bangor shed in North Wales in January 1958. Destined for the scrapyard, it was saved by shedmaster Mr J.M. Dunn, who organised the raising of funds to buy her. In 1973 the engine moved from Penrhyn Castle to Dinting where it was restored to working order.

Preserved Royal Scot Class 4-6-0 No.6115 *Scots Guardsman* gives brake van rides at Dinting. This engine made its first main line run in preservation on 2 September 1978 when it undertook a loaded test run from Dinting to Sheffield and back. On 14 October that year, *Guardsman* hauled the Anniversary Express from Guide Bridge to York and back; the tour having been organised to celebrate the tenth anniversary of the Dinting Railway Centre. After this the engine was confined to Dinting as BR would only issue a main line boiler certificate until 31 December 1978 because *Guardsman* needed its superheater flues replacing.

A busy day at Dinting.

The electrified Manchester–Sheffield–Wath route was already under threat of closure when it suffered three accidents within four months. The first took place on 10 March 1981, when an Arpley–Tinsley freight derailed as it was approaching Dinting Station. The overheads were brought down and considerable damage was done to the Up line and Up platform. The introduction of single line working over the Down between Hadfield and Dinting enabled freight trains to start running again that same day, but a bus replacement service operated for passengers until diesel multiple units were introduced a couple of days later.

Our pictures show the accident of 8 April when at 0245hrs, the Barton–Immingham anhydrous ammonia tank train hauled by Class 76 electrics Nos.76025 and 76027 derailed on a crossover at the west end of Hadfield Station. Ironically, freight trains had only been using this crossover since the March accident as BR had effectively single-tracked the Hadfield–Dinting section rather than spend any money on it.

2-8-0 No.63573 on a Down goods near Hadfield on 19 April 1952. (C.M. & J.M. Bentley)

Thompson B1 4-6-0 No.61170 on a Down express at Torside crossing on 15 August 1953. (C.M. & J.M. Bentley)

Three-cylinder Class V2 2-6-2 No.60820 at Crowden with an Up express on 15 August 1953. (C.M. & J.M. Bentley)

Woodhead Station on 18 December 1963.

Woodhead Station in March 1964.

The old single bore tunnels at Woodhead in 1957. The plan had been to put the overhead electric wires through these tunnels and, prior to the outbreak of war, line masts had been erected right up to the tunnel portals. However, a post-war survey found the bores to be in a sorry state; in some places the tunnel walls were bulging inwards. Though essential repairs were undertaken, engineering consultants Sir William Halcrow & Partners recommended to the LNER that a new twin bore tunnel be made.

Woodhead in the snow on 9 April 1983.

Severe weather conditions during the early months of 1940 played havoc with road, rail and canal transport. Here, troops are helping to clear snow on the Woodhead Route. As the picture also shows, the gantries for the overhead electric wires are in place.

Great Central Railway Class 2A 4-4-0 No.689 at Penistone at some time prior to the end of the First World War. Designed by Thomas Parker, the Class 2 & 2A 4-4-0s were built in batches between 1887 and 1893. At first they were used to haul Manchester to Kings Cross expresses as far as Grantham and back, but they were soon displaced by more advanced engines and were relegated to hauling local services and stopping trains. Some of these turns saw them working as far south as Leicester.

This is how the area around Penistone Station used to look, with the massive bulk of the Cammell Laird steelworks filling the background. The works were closed during the interwar slump as part of a strategy to reduce steelmaking and shipbuilding capacity throughout the country. Other victims included Palmers at Jarrow, a massive shipbuilding, marine engine manufacturing and iron and steelmaking complex. In all cases the owners were compensated, while the workers were left to fend for themselves or face trying to claim means-tested benefits of a few shillings a week.

Once an important junction for the Great Central Railway, Penistone was a crossroads for lines to Manchester, Sheffield, Barnsley and Huddersfield, and a number of trains started from and terminated here. It was also the scene of several railway accidents.

On 27 February 1927 the signalman at Penistone allowed LMS 2-4-2T No.10760 out on to the main line, having already accepted a Manchester Central to Marylebone express. Having turned on the turntable, the tank engine was now in the process of returning to its train to Huddersfield when the signalman cleared the signals for the express hauled by 4-4-0 No.5437 *Prince George*. The engine driver mistook the signals as being for him, and proceeded in the Sheffield direction in order to clear a set of points which, after being reversed, would send No.10670 back to its train. The fireman of the tank engine spotted the express hurtling towards them, warned his driver and promptly bailed out. To his credit, the driver of the tank engine opened up the regulator to increase speed, thereby reducing the impact.

MANCHESTER, PENISTONE, BARNSLEY, SHEFFIELD and MEXBOROUGH

Week Days

	a.m	a.m	a.m	a.m	a.m RC	a.m	a.m	a.m R	p.m S	a.m	p.m E	p.m S	p.m S	p.m	p.m RC
Manchester (Cen) dp	..	..	..	..	..	..	..	10 25	..	..	..	..	..	1 45	..
Manchester (L. Rd.) dep	1245	1 25	1 30	..	8 30	9 10	1010	10‡19	..	11 30	1240	1240	..	1‡45	2 16
Guide Bridge .... dep	..	..	..	..	8 39	9 19	1019	10 55	..	11 39	1249	1249	..	2 13	2 24
Dinting	..	..	..	..	..	9 30	1030	..	..	11 52	1 0	1 0	..	..	..
Glossop (Cen.) .. dep	..	..	..	..	..	9 7	10 7	..	..	11 37	1237	1237	..	..	..
Hadfield	Mondays only	..	..	..	..	9 34	..	..	..	..	..	..	..	..	..
Woodhead		..	..	..	..	..	..	..	..	..	Bb	..	..	..	..
Dunford Bridge		..	..	..	..	9 47	..	..	..	..	1 19	1 15	..	..	..
Penistone		2 3	..	6 55	9 6	9 54	1050	11 26	12 3	12 12	1 26	1 22	2 10	..	2 48
Silkstone .... arr		..	..	..	9 32	..	..	..	..	12S27	2 22	2 4	..	..	..
Barnsley (C.H.) ... "		2 24	..	..	9 45	..	..	..	..	12S42	2 38	2 17	..	..	..
Mexborough ..... "		2 45	..	..	10 15	..	..	..	..	..	..	..	..	..	..
Deepcar .... arr		..	..	7 2	..	..	..	..	1210	..	..	..	2 17	..	..
Oughty Bridge ...... "		..	..	7 7	..	..	..	..	1215	..	..	..	2 22	..	..
Wadsley Bridge ..... "	..	..	..	7 11	..	..	..	..	1219	..	..	..	2 26	..	..
Sheffield (Victoria) . "	1 32	..	2 43	7 16	9 25	10 14	11 6	11 42	1224	12 28	1 43	1 38	2 31	2 53	3 6
Rotherham (Cen.). arr	..	..	4 31	..	10u11	..	..	11 58	..	12S51	2 58	2 58	..	..	4 26
Mexborough ..... "	..	..	4 45	..	..	..	..	12 13	..	1 S7	3 12	3 12	..	..	4 45

Week Days—continued / **Sundays**

	p.m	p.m RC	p.m E	p.m	p.m	p.m R	p.m	p.m	p.m E	p.m S	p.m	Sun a.m	a.m	a.m	a.m RC	a.m L	p.m	p.m RC	p.m	p.m	p.m
Manchester (Cen) dp	..	..	..	..	..	5 35	..	..	..	..	10 40	..	..	..	..	1032	..	..	..	5 30	..
Manchester (L. Rd.) dep	..	4 5	..	5 0	..	5‡45	6 38	8 33	1035	10 35	10‡45	1 25	8 35	9 40	1035	..	1235	4 10	4 35	5‡35	8 40
Guide Bridge .... dep	..	4 14	..	5 9	..	6 [illegible]	6 48	8 42	1050	10 50	11 10	1 33	8 44	9 52	1044	11 0	1244	4 19	4 44	5 58	8 49
Dinting	..	..	..	5 17	..	..	..	..	..	..	..	..	8 58	10 4	..	..	1259	..	4 58	..	9 0
Glossop (Cen.) .. dep	..	..	..	5 7	..	..	6T49	8T19	..	10T19	..	..	8 37	9T49	..	..	1237	..	4T49	..	8T49
Hadfield	..	..	..	..	..	..	7 7	8 53	..	11 3	..	..	..	10 8	..	..	..	..	5 2	..	9 4
Woodhead	..	..	..	..	..	..	..	..	..	11 15	..	..	..	..	..	..	..	..	..	..	..
Dunford Bridge	..	..	..	5 31	..	..	7 23	..	..	..	11S34	..	..	10 21	..	..	..	..	5 13	..	9 16
Penistone	[illegible]	4 42	5 12	5 39	6 20	6 37	7 30	9 12	1121	11 27	11 39	1 59	9 18	10 29	1117	1132	1 19	4 52	5 21	6 25	9 23
Silkstone .... arr	..	4 57	..	6 14	..	..	..	10E17	..	..	..	..	..	..	..	..	..	..	..	..	..
Barnsley (C.H.) ... "	..	5 10	..	6 27	..	..	..	10E32	..	..	..	2 45	..	..	..	..	..	..	..	..	..
Mexborough ..... "	..	5 31	..	..	..	..	..	..	..	..	..	3 6	..	..	..	..	..	..	..	..	..
Deepcar .... arr	4 33	..	5 19	..	6 27	..	7 39	..	..	..	..	..	..	..	..	..	..	..	..	..	..
Oughty Bridge ...... "	4 38	..	5 24	..	6 32	..	..	..	..	..	..	..	..	..	..	..	..	..	..	..	..
Wadsley Bridge ..... "	4 42	..	5 28	..	6 36	..	7 46	..	..	..	..	..	..	10 52	..	..	..	..	5 42	..	9 36
Sheffield (Victoria) . "	4 47	4 58	5 33	5 55	6 41	6 53	7 51	9 30	1142	11 47	12 0	2 15	9 44	10 57	1143	1158	1 45	5 18	5 49	6 41	9 41
Rotherham (Cen.). arr	..	5 31	..	6 32	..	7 18	9u1	..	..	..	..	3 33	1023	..	..	1214	2 53	5 39	..	6 57	..
Mexborough ..... "	..	..	..	6 46	..	7 31	9 15	..	..	..	..	..	1035	..	..	1227	4 25	5 54	..	7 10	..

Week Days

	a.m	a.m	a.m	a.m	a.m	a.m S	a.m R	a.m	p.m S	p.m	p.m E	p.m S	p.m	p.m E
Mexborough ..... dep	..	..	7 58	..	8 48	..	10 48	..	..	12E29	..	1259	2 22	..
Rotherham (Cen.). "	..	..	8 13	..	9 5	..	11 0	11 38	..	12E45	..	1 15	2 39	..
Sheffield (Victoria) . dep	2 50	8 15	8 44	9 5	9 52	1045	11 19	12 11	1255	1 16	2 12	2 12	3 27	4 10
Wadsley Bridge ..... "	..	8 20	..	..	..	1050	..	..	1 0	..	RC	RC	..	4 15
Oughty Bridge ...... "	Except Mondays	8 24	..	..	..	1054	..	..	1 4	..	..	..	..	4 19
Deepcar .... "		8 31	..	..	..	1059	..	..	1 9	..	..	..	..	4 24
Mexborough ..... dep		..	..	..	..	..	..	..	..	..	..	..	..	..
Barnsley (C.H.) ... "		..	8 10	..	..	..	10S40	..	..	..	1 22	1 15	..	..
Silkstone .... "		..	8 26	..	..	..	10S51	..	..	..	1 33	1 26	..	..
Penistone		8 40	9 8	9 22	10 8	11 8	11 37	12 28	1 17	..	2 29	2 29	3 45	4 32
Dunford Bridge		..	..	9 30	..	..	..	12 36	..	..	..	..	3 53	..
Woodhead		..	..	9 35	..	..	..	..	..	..	..	..	..	..
Hadfield	..	..	9 23	..	10 27	..	..	..	..	..	..	..	..	..
Glossop (Cen.) .. arr	5U51	..	10T3	1014	11T3	..	..	1 14	..	..	..	..	4 14	..
Dinting	5U41	..	..	9 47	10 29	..	..	12 48	..	..	..	..	4 6	..
Guide Bridge ...... arr	3 40	..	9 33	9 59	10 39	..	12 5	12 59	..	1 58	3 0	3 0	4 16	..
Manchester (L. Rd.). arr	3 53	..	10‡5	10 9	10 48	..	12‡35	1 9	..	2‡35	3 10	3 10	4 25	..
Manchester (Cen) ar	..	..	9 58	..	..	..	12 30	..	..	2 31	..	..	..	..

Week Days—continued / **Sundays**

	p.m RC	p.m	p.m	p.m R	p.m RC	p.m	p.m E	p.m S	Sun a.m	a.m	a.m	a.m	a.m	p.m RC	p.m	p.m L	p.m	p.m RC	p.m
Mexborough ..... dep	..	..	..	5 53	6 39	7 45	..	..	..	..	8 30	1054	1154	..	2 49	5 54	..	..	9 5
Rotherham (Cen.). "	..	..	..	6 8	6 54	8 1	9 30	9 30	..	..	8 45	11 8	12 8	..	3 2[illegible]	6 8	..	..	9 18
Sheffield (Victoria) . dep	4 32	5 20	5 30	6 37	7 24	9 8	1033	1033	2 55	6 35	9 35	1127	1235	2 23	4 30	6 27	7 30	8 31	9 50
Wadsley Bridge ..... "	..	..	5 35	..	..	..	..	..	..	6 41	9 40	..	..	..	..	..	7 35	..	..
Oughty Bridge ...... "	..	..	5 39	..	..	..	..	..	..	..	..	..	..	..	..	..	..	..	..
Deepcar .... "	..	..	5 44	..	..	..	..	..	..	..	..	..	..	..	..	..	..	..	..
Mexborough ..... dep	..	..	..	..	..	..	9 57	9 57	..	..	..	..	..	..	..	..	..	..	..
Barnsley (C.H.) ... "	4E0	4S50	..	6 15	..	..	1023	1023	..	..	..	..	..	..	..	..	..	..	..
Silkstone .... "	4E11	5S 1	..	6 26	..	..	1033	1033	..	..	..	..	..	..	..	..	..	..	..
Penistone	4 54	5 37	5 52	6 55	7 42	9 27	1050	1050	..	7 2	9 59	1144	1252	2 40	4 52	6 44	7 52	8 48	10 7
Dunford Bridge	..	..	..	7 3	..	..	..	..	..	..	10 7	..	..	..	..	6 53	8 2	..	..
Woodhead	..	..	..	..	..	..	..	Vv	..	..	..	..	..	..	..	..	..	..	..
Hadfield	..	..	..	..	..	..	..	..	..	7 24	10 18	..	1 15	..	..	..	8 13	..	..
Glossop (Cen.) .. arr	5 44	6 14	..	..	8 14	1014	1114	1114	..	7T33	10T33	..	1T33	..	5 44	..	8T33	9y44	1044
Dinting	5 17	5 56	..	..	8 1	9 47	11 9	11 9	..	7 26	10 21	..	1 17	..	5 11	..	8 16	Zz	1026
Guide Bridge ...... arr	5 30	6 6	..	7 28	8 13	10 0	1118	1118	3 48	7 40	10 36	1221	1 32	3 17	5 27	7 14	8 26	9 21	1039
Manchester (L. Rd.). arr	5 40	6 16	..	8‡F0	8 23	10 9	1128	1128	4 0	7 55	10 50	1‡ 5	1 46	3 31	5 43	7‡58	8 39	9 31	1051
Manchester (Cen) ar	..	..	..	7 53	..	..	..	..	..	..	..	1251	..	..	..	7 41	..	..	..

Bb Calls at Woodhead 1 14 pm on Weds,. Thurs. and Fris.
E or E Except Saturdays
F 5 minutes later on Saturdays

L Light Refreshments available between Manchester (Central), Sheffield and Mexborough
R Refreshment Car between Manchester (Central), Sheffield and Mexborough
RC Refreshment Car between Manchester and Sheffield

S or S Saturdays only
T Change at Hadfield
U Arrival times. Via Godley Jn.
u 3 minutes *earlier* on Saturdays
Vv Stops at 11 1 pm to set down on informing Guard at Sheffield

y Change at Dinting and inform Guard at Penistone
Zz Stops at 9 9 pm when required to set down on informing Guard at Penistone
‡ Change at Guide Bridge

Penistone Station on a cold January day in 1966.

Penistone in the snow in January 1974.

A diesel-hauled passenger train passes through Penistone.

On 21 April 1981, the Locomotive Club of Great Britain (North West) ran what was probably the last electric-hauled passenger over the Woodhead Route. The train, hauled by No.76025, is pictured at Penistone as it travels toward Sheffield.

Whilst waiting for the LCGB special passenger train, the *Sheffield Star* photographer snapped this pair of Class 76s doing their stuff. By 1980, there were 40 trains a day using Woodhead – about one-third of its capacity – and officials higher up were of the opinion that the £44 million needed to convert the route to BR's standard 25kV system would be a waste of assets. What had been the first railway route across the Pennines closed without fuss on 24 July 1981.

By early 1983 the only regular railway activity passing through Sheffield Victoria Station were the Huddersfield diesel multiple units going to or coming back from reversal at Nunnery. On 16 May, a new Penistone to Sheffield Midland service via Barnsley came into operation, thanks to a subsidy from the South Yorkshire Passenger Transport Executive.

By January 1955, Wortley station's chances of staying open were slim. With the number of people using it on a daily basis averaging out at less than 20, BR had declared it uneconomical and its future was about to be decided by the Transport Users' Consultative Committee.

Porter Lidgett of Outbridge mans the ticket office at Wortley Station.

Officially opened on 15 September 1851, Victoria Station was positively palatial when compared to the Midland's offering at Wicker. Approached from Blonk Street by way of a 350-yard-long road, Victoria's 400ft frontage was faced with Greenmore stone and ashlar. There was one main platform 1000ft by 40ft, with bays at either end. Rain water was collected from the roof and used for flushing the station's toilets.

The Royal Victoria Hotel adjoining Victoria Station was Sheffield's finest hotel in the late Victorian and Edwardian eras. In 1910 the cheapest rooms cost 4s a night, luncheon 2s 6d and dinner 5s.

LNER Class D10 No.5437 *Prince George* pulls out of Victoria with an east-bound stopper on 14 September 1929. Built by the Great Central Railway, these Class 11E engines were better known as the 'Directors' because they carried names of those who had sat on the managing board of the company.

This particular engine was built at Gorton in 1913 as No.437 *Charles Stuart-Wortley* but was renamed Prince George in around 1920, in honour of the youngest surviving child of King George V and Queen Mary. Charles Stuart-Wortley served as a director of the GCR from 1897 to 1922 and was created Baron Stuart of Wortley in 1916. (W.L. Good courtesy the Gordon Coltas Photographic Trust)

Between March 1903 and August 1905, 40 Class 9K 4-4-2Ts were built for the GCR for working suburban passenger trains out of Marylebone, but when more powerful engines became available a large number of them were transferred north. All passed into LNER ownership, becoming their Class C13 and having 5000 added to their numbers. No.6055 was one of the first batch to be built and was constructed by the Vulcan Foundry at Newton-le-Willows. (W.L. Good courtesy the Gordon Coltas Photographic Trust)

4-4-0s Nos.689–693 comprised the GCR's Class 2A and were built in the company shops at Gorton in 1894. When this picture was taken at Sheffield Victoria in 1929 No.691 had become LNER Class D7 No.5691. A picture of one of this class taken at Penistone appears earlier in the book. The main differences are the elegant Robinson chimney in place of the original stovepipe and a Belpaire firebox in place of the roundtop boiler. No.5691 was withdrawn in 1933. (W.L. Good courtesy Gordon Coltas Photographic Trust)

Members of the Sheffield Home Guard parade at Victoria Station prior to their trip to London, where they will take part in the Stand-Down Parade.

Modernisation in the form of fluorescent lighting comes to Victoria Station in 1953.

The carriages of *The Master Cutler* are readied for use on 20 January 1953.

In April 1959 the Staybrite Works of Firth-Vickers Stainless Steels Ltd manufactured a new headboard for *The Master Cutler*. The board was presented to the Master Cutler, Mr J. Hugh Neill, by Firth-Vickers Chairman, Mr W.D. Pugh. The Master Cutler then presented the headboard to BR Eastern Region Traffic Manager, Mr S. Fiennes. From left to right: Mr W.D. Pugh, Mr S. Fiennes, and Mr J. Hugh Neill.

Sir Brian Robertson, BTC Chairman, chats with the driver prior to the departure from Sheffield Victoria of the first scheduled electric passenger train. The train had originated from Kings Cross, hauled by A4 streamlined Pacific No.60008 *Dwight D Eisenhower*. It took 2hrs 51mins to reach Sheffield, where the steam locomotive was detached and replaced by electric locomotive No.27000.

The first electric-hauled revenue earning passenger train departs Sheffield Victoria on 14 September 1954, having been whistled away by Sir Brian Robertson at 1145hrs. It reached Manchester London Road less than one hour later on what was for passengers the first ever smoke-free trip through Woodhead Tunnel. The full electric service commenced six days later, the fastest scheduled trains doing the trip to Manchester in just 51 minutes. The Manchester–Sheffield electric loco fleet enabled capacity on the line to be increased by 50 per cent, and as each loco spent only two hours on shed every five days the fleet could do the work of 110 steam locomotives.

Ernest Hales on duty as the night left luggage attendant at Victoria on 30 December 1957.

Class EM2 electric *Ariadne* at Victoria in 1960. Under BR's new TOPS classification code for electric locomotives, the Manchester–Sheffield EM1 Bo+Bos Nos.26000–26067 became Class 76 and the EM2 Co-Cos Nos.27000–27006 were designated Class 77. The later models were withdrawn in one fell swoop before they could be renumbered. (C.M. & J.M. Bentley)

From 13 June 1962, British Railways raised the meal prices for *table d'hôte* by what was then a substantial amount. Breakfast went up from 7s 6d to 8s; lunch from 9s 6d to 11s; afternoon tea from 3s to 3s 6d and dinner from 10s to 12s. Whilst unlikely to affect business travellers, the fact that these increases were on top of a rise in fares was thought to be sufficient to drive away other passengers. Our picture from 1962 shows Mr W. Powell, Leading Attendant on the Sheffield–Harwich service.

The holder of the world speed record for steam traction, *Mallard*, is seen here being hauled through Victoria on 25 February 1964, en route to Clapham Museum.

This picture of a deserted Victoria was taken on 2 January 1970 to use with stories about the axing of the Manchester–Sheffield electric services.

As the lady from the bookstall looks on, station staff shut the gates at Victoria in this picture taken on 2 January 1970. Incidentally, in 1989 the W H Smith bookstall at Manchester Victoria was donated to the Severn Valley Railway, where it was restored to its original condition.

VICTORIA STATION

Sheffield Victoria came to life again in March 1973 when Midland closed as part of the modernisation programme. Suitably attired against the weather, the station announcer was in fine voice. He had to be, as all he had was a hand-held loudhailer.

The last electric passenger service out of Sheffield departs for Manchester on 5 January 1970... or does it? This picture, like some of the previous ones, was in fact taken three days earlier. After 5 January the only passenger services operating out of Victoria were those to Penistone and Huddersfield.

Once upon a time, the summer months would have seen Victoria crowded with holiday makers. This is how it looked on 23 August 1974.

Demolition work starts on the frontage of Victoria Station.

By May 1981 the demolition work was well underway.

Woodburn Junction, or more correctly Woodbourne Junction, opened to traffic in August 1864. In doing so, it enabled the South Yorkshire Railway to switch its operations from the Midland Station at Wicker to the Manchester, Sheffield & Lincoln's much grander Sheffield Victoria. The signalbox is situated between the main line and what had been the LNWR City Goods branch.

Darnall Station – or Darnal as it was called until 1887 – opened in February 1849. It is one of the oldest surviving stations in the area, although it has been reduced in status to an unstaffed halt. The island platform layout came about during the 1920s when the LNER quadrupled the track, the two inner tracks being used for passenger trains.

D5656 is seen here en route to London at the head of *The Master Cutler* on 4 April 1962. One of these Brush Type 2s was recorded on the Sheffield Pullman service for the first time on 16 June 1960, when D5589 headed the 1520hrs to Kings Cross. On the previous occasion it had been hauled by Peppercorn A2 No.60533.

SEND IT BY RAIL

This picture from December 1957 gives some idea of the vast quantities of parcels traffic once carried on the railway. Here, station staff load a night parcels train on platform 3 at Victoria.

In 1986, *The Star* was invited to photograph the working of a south-bound night mail train. Their guinea pig for the adventure was reporter Martin Dawes, seen here posting a letter in the mailbox on the train.

A few minutes later the hard work began as mail sacks were heaved on board.

Once the train had departed, the sacks were opened and the task of sorting began. Nowadays, part of the security for trains carrying 'sensitive' goods such as mail or nuclear waste is addressed in the rules and regulations for drivers and signallers. For example, if a mail train comes to a stand at a stop signal, the driver immediately contacts the signaller. If the signaller knows of no reason why the train has come to a stand it is immediately treated as suspicious and the police are alerted.

Martin's letter gets franked.

The work of sorting begins.

From 1 February 1958, the whole of the Sheffield area came under the control of British Railways Eastern Region and soon rationalisation plans were being drawn up to rid the area of its many of goods yards and locomotive depots. A modernisation programme – which included the elimination of steam traction – would sweep away these locations and replace them with one freight terminal, one marshalling yard and one locomotive depot. Grimesthorpe locomotive depot was chosen as the location for a new freight terminal. This picture – taken on 26 July 1965 – shows the Sundries Shed at the terminal after it had opened for business. The 920ft shed was equipped to be able to deal with dozens of vans and wagons at one time. (British Railways Eastern Region)

This image, taken on 30 September 1965, shows some of the equipment used in the shed. Grimesthorpe's handling capacity of around 700 tons of goods per day was sufficient for BR to close the goods depots at Blast Lane, West Tinsley, Wharf Street, Bridgehouses and Wicker. (British Railways Eastern Region)

If Grimesthorpe Freight Terminal needed a landmark, this was it: the Goliath crane. (British Railways Eastern Region)

Here an electromagnet is being used to lift steel billets. (British Railways Eastern Region)

Timber traffic dominates this busy scene at Wharf Street goods yard in 1959.

Queens Road goods depot plays host to row after row of 16-ton four-wheel mineral wagons. In February 1948, the Ideal Stocks Committee was established to consider the types of goods vehicles that ought to be developed. Their report, published two years later, recommended that wooden bodied coal wagons should be phased out as soon as possible, and replaced with modern steel ones and soon over 50,000 16 tonners were on order. The Committee intended the 16 tonner to be nothing more than a stopgap until BR and industry had upgraded their handling facilities to accommodate larger vehicles.

Also in the picture are a number of Scammell Scarab three-wheeler tractor units, famed for their amazing turning circles. Railwaymen only needed a provisional licence to be able to get behind the wheel of these machines, as BR's own accredited examiners were authorised to issue certificates of competency to successful candidates.

Prior to rationalisation there were nine goods depots in and around Sheffield. Of these, the former Lincolnshire, Derbyshire & East Coast Railway facility at Attercliffe dealt mainly with timber, Blast Lane with coal traffic and perishables, park goods also dealt with coal traffic while Bridgehouses (pictured here in May 1962) and Wharf Street concentrated on perishables.

The Queens Road, West Tinsley and the Wicker depots dealt with general traffic, while Pond Street processed wagon loads for collection only. Between them, Bridgehouses, Queens Road and Wicker shifted nearly 30,000 tons of sundries a month. Pond Street was closed in October 1961, Queens Road in May 1963 and Park Goods the following October.

These two pictures, taken during the guards' strike in March 1966, show some of the various types of goods vehicles then in service. They include: open merchandise wooden-bodied five-plank drop-door wagons; 16-ton steel mineral wagons of which over 200,000 were built between 1950 and 1958; a BR standard 20-ton brake van which was based on a LNER long wheelbase design introduced in 1929 for use on fast freights; and three Prestflow cement wagons. Over 1800 Prestflows were built; they were gravity loaded but discharged using compressed air. Some were later adapted to carry salt or power station fly ash.

This spectacular picture of flames pouring out of the Wicker depot on 31 July 1966 was taken by *Star* reader Mr Askew of Pitsmoor. Originally built as the terminus of the Sheffield & Rotherham Railway, Wicker opened on 1 November 1838.

With the transfer of passenger services to Sheffield New Midland Station in February 1870, Wicker became a goods depot. Its passing as a passenger station wasn't missed; it was once described as 'a miserable little station, hideous, dirty, dilapidated and unattractive'. The Midland spent a small fortune on the place over the years, including over £100,000 in the 1890s, to enable it to cope with increasing goods traffic. It closed in July 1965, a victim of the rationalisation of freight facilities in the city. (Mr Askew)

A firefighter, overcome by the effects of smoke inhalation, is helped to safety.

The casualty clearing station: basic to say the least.

Damping down operations continue.

Once the fire was out, the investigation into its cause began. Here, British Transport Police take stock of the devastation.

This is the Sheffield car ferry terminal in May 1968. Normally, George Collins would have driven the vehicle onto the train himself, but for the benefit of this *Star* picture, he was persuaded to guide it on.

On 3 January 1961, *The Star* was invited along to a demonstration of a new type of road-rail vehicle at Bridgehouses goods depot. The demo was a joint effort between British Road Services and British Railways, displaying wagons capable of taking an 11-ton load, though it was anticipated that wagons of all types would be available when the service went live. By the end of January, BR had 300 wagons on order.

The vehicles themselves were a joint development between British Railways and the Pressed Steel Co of Cowley, Oxford. The concept was to combine the flexibility of road transport with the speed and economies of scale offered by rail. It was envisaged that the scheme would allow any Sheffield customer to load road-railers at their own premises, and providing they had been driven over to the nearest railhead by 6.00pm, BR would guarantee overnight forwarding by rail for delivery by road the next morning to almost any part of the country.

The close-up of the wheel system shows a wagon in rail mode. The road wheels were raised and lowered by hydraulics. (British Railways Eastern Region)

Ickles freightliner terminal, seen here under construction in May 1967. It opened
a couple of months later with services to Glasgow, Kings Cross and Cardiff.

On 29 October 1965, Lord Beeching unveiled this plaque to mark the official opening of Tinsley marshalling yard. Depending on one's point of view, Dr Richard Beeching is either the saviour of Britain's railways or its butcher in the pay of the road transport lobby. By the time he was appointed chairman of the newly created British Railways Board, closures were already occurring, as BR struggled under the pressures of an eye-watering deficit.

Interestingly, for the first five years of its existence BR had run at a profit. However, that was torpedoed by the Tory Government of the day when it pushed through the 1953 Transport Act. In one go the Act decentralised the railway network by handing too much power to the individual Regions. At the same time, while the Act encouraged competition between different forms of transport, British Railways was denied the opportunity to take on road transport on a level playing field because a multitude of charges, conditions, liabilities were imposed upon it, as well as having to suffer political and Treasury interference.

It was only after the Act came into force that BR begin to accumulate losses, but matters weren't helped by a 17-day strike by ASLEF members in 1955, causing many freight customers to switch to road transport permanently. The deficit reached £16.5 million by 1956 and two years later it was £48.1 million. By 1960 it hit £67.7 million and in 1981 it reached £86.5 million, culminating in 1962 a staggering £104 million.

Prior to the Beeching Report, British Railways operated over some 17,830 route miles of lines. However, the report, based on a series of traffic surveys carried out during the weekend of 23 April 1961, found that of this, nearly 6000 miles were carrying just one per cent of passengers and one per cent of freight. Although with hindsight it is easy to see flaws in the survey, at the time it was felt that something had to be done, and quickly.

Beeching proposed that the railway should concentrate its efforts on providing good, reliable inter-city services, commuter trains, and bulk freight and container services at the expense of uneconomic rural branch lines whose communities might be better served by buses or private motorcars.

There were to be some big casualties. Beeching recommended closure of the Settle and Carlisle line, the Waverley route, the Somerset & Dorset and the Great Central Main Line. He also recommended closing the Hope Valley line between Manchester and Sheffield in favour of the electrified Woodhead route, which he believed was an example of the railway at its best. Some 2128 stations were listed for closure and on the day the report was published the BBC solemnly read out the names of every one of them. By 1965 BR had reduced its manpower by 20 per cent, and by 1969 the network had been cut back to 13,261 route miles.

What we have to remember is that Beeching did not close lines himself, he only made recommendations, and local communities and authorities had a chance of keeping lines open if they so wished. Many chose not to act, and have since paid the price.

From an operational point of view, Tinsley Yard's last connection with the national network was at Shepcote Lane which was laid during the summer of 1964.

Journalists were invited along to Tinsley marshalling yard on 27 October 1975 for a look round the BR's TOPS (Total Operations Processing System) office there. The visit coincided with the system going live throughout the railway network.

TOPS is computer system for recording movements and locations of all locomotives and rolling stock on the network. A modern TOPS list for a freight train will give headcode, locomotive number, wagon numbers in running order in the train, whether or not there are any dangerous goods being carried and so on. It can provide information such all wagons currently in a marshalling yard, or all locomotives at a traction maintenance depot.

Once the system was fully operational it reduced the number of wagons getting 'lost' on the network. This sometimes happened when the wagon docket – a card ticket giving details of whether the wagon was empty, loaded or crippled as well as its destination – parted company with the wagon.

TOPS operators Lawrence Holland, Robert Whitham and Eirleen Thompson, at work at Tinsley marshalling yard on 27 October 1975. The guys on the ground making up the trains would phone or fax a list of wagon numbers, in the order of position in the train, to TOPS. Trains could not be released to traffic until this had been done.

Right: It soon became apparent that Tinsley Yard needed more powerul shunting engines than the standard BR Class 08 0-6-0DE type. The answer was to permanently couple a pair of 08s into a master and slave unit of 700bhp. Three of these units were created and became BR Class 13 No 13001-13003. As all driving was done from the master, the slave units had their cabs removed. In the picture, we have the master unit nearest the camera, with the cabless slave unit beyond it.

Tinsley Yard had an operational life of less than 20 years.

Nothing moves at Tinsley on 17 January 1985 as BR staff stage a
one-day stoppage to show solidarity with striking miners.

The derelict Tinsley East signalbox.

English Electric Type 3 diesel-electrics were holding the fort at Wath Yard when the *Star* photographer turned up on 23 February 1968. The picture was taken for a story announcing the yard was under threat of closure.

When first opened by the Great Central Railway in 1907, Wath Yard was the biggest of its type in the country. Wath was a hump marshalling yard which used gravity instead of locomotives to marshal wagons into trains. It worked by pushing a rake of coal wagons along towards the sidings, on a track that gently rose to a crest (the hump) with a steep slope on the far side. As the train was pushed over the hump, wagons were uncoupled from one another and allowed to run downhill under force of gravity. Shunters would then have time to alter points, allowing individual wagons onto the correct track where their train was being assembled.

Designed by Great Central Chief Mechanical Engineer John George Robinson, the 'Wath Daisies' were four massive 0-8-4 tank engines built between December 1908 and January 1909 for hump shunting at the new marshalling yard at Wath-on-Dearne. With an overall length in excess of 45ft, weighing 99 tons when in full working order, and with a tractive effort of over 34,000lb, they were the heaviest and most powerful tank engines in the country.

Designated Class 8H by the GCR, the 'Daisies' held a number of firsts in British railway locomotive design. They were the first 0-8-4 wheel arrangement locomotives to be built to work in Britain and the first shunting engines in the country to be equipped with three cylinders. As can be seen in the photograph, the outside cylinders had their drive connected to the third coupled axle, whereas the inside cylinder was connected to the second axle.

Another feature was that they were fitted with oval buffers. This was a late design change by Robinson, and was done to reduce buffer lock when the engine was propelling a long rake of goods wagons towards the crest of the hump. During 1932 Sir Nigel Gresley fitted No.6171 with a booster unit in order to increase its tractive effort as there were occasions, especially during bad weather, when it was necessary for two 'Daisies' to work together in order to get heavy trains over the hump.

Two additional 'Daisies', complete with booster equipment, were built by the LNER at Gorton Works during 1932 and all six locomotives survived into BR ownership as Nos.69900–69905. During the early 1950s, their work was taken over by diesels and the engines ended up at Doncaster, though No.69903 soon paid the price of failing to impress. When she was sent on trial to Immingham Docks but was found to be unsuited to the task, she was turned into saucepans. Nos.69901 and 69905 were eventually sent to Frodingham while the other three lingered on for a while at Doncaster, finding occasional work dragging long lines of locomotives around the Plant. This didn't last long, and the remaining three were condemned in 1956. (Collection Clive Hardy)

LNER Class U1 2-8-0+0-8-2 No.2395 was the first Beyer Garratt type articulated locomotive to be built for a British main line railway company, although the Great Central Railway had toyed with the idea prior to the First World War. The LNER had a specific role for this locomotive in mind: to bank heavy coal trains out from Wath up the 1 in 40 Worsborough Incline between Wentworth and Silkstone Junctions.

Manufacturers Beyer, Peacock & Co of Gorton, Manchester, worked on the design details with the LNER's Chief Mechanical Engineer, Nigel Gresley. The final assembly of this 178 ton, 87ft long monster was completed in just 20 days so that it could take part in the 1925 Stockton & Darlington Railway Centenary celebrations.

Within a year of its entering service in July 1925, No.2395 was in Doncaster Works for retubing after the water at Worsborough had rapidly corroded the tubes and stays. Although it was not pure, the water was too soft, leaving hardly any build-up of protective scale deposits on the inside of the boiler. Three years later, the engine was back in Doncaster, this time for heavy repairs, following the discovery that the firebox roof stays were badly corroded.

By 1949 the boiler had only a few years left on the clock, but with the electrification of the Woodhead–Wath route going ahead, BR were reluctant to order a replacement unless alternative work could be found for the brute. On 7 March 1949 No.69999, as she now was, arrived at Bromsgrove in the West Midlands for banking duties on the 1 in 37.7 Lickey Incline. It was not a success, and after a couple of years the engine was to be found in store at Mexborough. After this came another year's work on the Worsborough Incline followed by a few more months in store, and in August 1952 a move to Gorton Works for conversion to oil firing and the fitting of a Stone's generator for an electric headlight. In the end the conversion was not considered a success and No.69999 was withdrawn in December 1955. (Collection Clive Hardy)

The remains of Wath Yard.

Introduced by the Great Central in 1911, Robinson's Class 8K 2-8-0 heavy freight engines quickly established such a reputation for reliability that during the First World War, the War Office ordered the construction of several hundred for service in France with the Railway Operating Division of the Royal Engineers. Having already built a batch of 50 8Ks for the Great Central in 1912, the lion's share of the WO order – 369 engines – went to the North British Locomotive Co of Glasgow. Other commercial manufacturers included Robert Stephenson & Co (82), Nasmyth Wilson (32), Kitson & Co (32) and the Great Central's Gorton Works (6 – 3 in 1918 and 3 in 1919). There is a rumour that the 1919 engines never left Gorton before their subsequent sale to the GCR for £6064 each. (Collection Clive Hardy)

A nuclear waste train passes through Rotherham on 29 September 1981.

South Yorkshire coal en route to a Notts power station.

Miners at Dearne Valley Pit celebrate breaking their own weekly output record in January 1977.

In 1887, the Railway Clearing House came up with a set of regulations aimed at standardising the construction of 8 and 10-ton private owner wagons. The regulations covered the wagon frame, wheels, brakes, axles and axleboxes, bearing springs and buffers, as well as limiting the wheelbase to not less than 7ft 6ins and not more than 9ft. Beyond that the private owners were allowed to build the body – these coal wagons photographed at Aldwarke Colliery, Rotherham, in March 1933, are of the six-plank variety – to suit their requirements.

Once these regulations had been introduced, no newly constructed private wagon – and there were thousands of them built by dozens of companies – could enter service until it had been inspected by the relevant main line railway's Wagon Superintendent. If the wagon conformed to the standard it was fitted with numbered registration plates, one on each side, and allowed to enter traffic.

When we talk about railways, most of us automatically think of the main line railways, but there was a time when hundreds of factories, mines and quarries had their own rail systems as well as iron and steel works, shipyards, docks and harbours. Some of these systems were very short; a few tens of yards long, the wagons were hauled by rope, pulled by horses, or even pushed along by hand. Others were extensive, running for many miles and often complete with full signalling and running rights for their locomotives over main lines.

Though the main focus of this picture is the 110-ton gun barrel, we can also see that Firth's operated both standard and narrow gauge systems within their works. The wagon supporting the gun barrel looks sturdy and is fitted with buffers, three-link couplings and even has brakes. In this period, that made it something of a 'luxury' model for this sort of job.

Once again, the focus of this picture isn't the railway wagon but the amount of punishment the plate from HMS *Lord Clyde* had withstood. Though from an earlier date than the Firth's internal user wagon, the Charles Camel & Co wagon is far more primitive, lacking brakes and couplings, and was probably pushed round the plant by brute force.

BSC2 is a part of Sheffield's railway heritage in that it was the first diesel locomotive to be built by the Yorkshire Engine Co. It was one of a pair of 0-4-0 diesel-electrics ordered by Steel, Peach & Toner for their Templeborough Steelworks at Rotherham, where it was employed hauling ingot casting cars around the melting shop. Declared surplus to requirements in 1982, the locomotive was acquired by the South Yorkshire Railway Preservation Society in 1987. In 2002 the society moved BSC2 to Peak Rail, Owsley. (Clive Hardy)

Coopers Metal, Brightside proved to be the end of the line for Woodhead Route 1500V DC Bubo electric locomotives Nos.76029, 76032, 76033 and 76044. The picture was taken on 23 March 1983.

Just one of the many steam locomotives to be scrapped in the Sheffield area.

ROTHERHAM, BARNSLEY, SWINTON AND DONCASTER

Sheffield to Rotherham at Meadowbank. (S. Duke)

Floodwater completely covers the tracks at Rotherham and Masbro' Station.

Flooding at Rotherham and Masbro' station on 4 September 1931. This
picture was sent to us by *Star* reader Mr J. M. Nelson of Broom Valley.

Mr C. Thomas, stationmaster of Rotherham Central, with a section of the 30-yard-long garden which had taken first prize in the 1956 British Railways district stations competition for the Doncaster Operating District of the Eastern Region. A riot of colour, the garden featured over 100 varieties of flowers and blooms including dahlias, hollyhocks, geraniums, sweat peas and asters. One rather ingenious feature which can be seen in this picture is the use of an old mirror to reflect a fish pond so as to give the impression that there was an aquarium set in the embankment. Having also won the 1955 competition, Mr Thomas and his staff were hoping to make it three-in-a-row in 1957.

A Stanier 8F 2-8-0 trundles past the blooms at Rotherham Central. It is August 1961 and once again the station has won the divisional garden competition.

Rotherham Masbro' complete with semaphore signals, locomotive water columns, and rusting glassless canopy. The date is 27 May 1964 and the Mayor of Rotherham is threatening to send a letter of complaint over the state of the station to the Chairman of BR, Lord Beeching.

A quiet moment at Rotherham Masbro' on 30 September 1981.

The official naming ceremony for InterCity 125 power car No.43047 *Rotherham Enterprise*, held at Rotherham Station, in March 1984. The Mayor, Councillor Allott receives the gift of a model of the 125 from Paul Watkinson, Divisional Manager Yorkshire Division BR after the ceremony.

Fitter Engleburt Klik works on Orient Express Pullman car *Lucille* at Thomas Hill (Rotherham) Ltd.

A diesel-hydraulic built by Thomas Hill at Peak Rail, Buxton, Derbyshire. The locomotive was there for a few days prior to onward delivery to its owners. (Baz Blood)

A diesel-hydraulic build by Thomas Hill at Peak Rail,
Rowsley South, on 25 September 2006. (Clive Hardy)

Never mind Virgin West Coast's *Pendolino* tilting trains, the technology
for those models actually originated in BR's Advance Passenger Train
programme of the 1970s. Here, scrap merchant Ken Booth poses with his
latest acquisition, APT power cars, following the cancellation of the project.

This picture of Barnsley Court House station was taken on 11 March 1959. It was published the following day with the news that it might soon be closed because of the upkeep costs of the viaduct approach. The station officially closed on 19 April 1960 though the last passenger train had been the 1830hrs to Sheffield on 15 April.

Though passenger services from Barnsley Court House station had ended in April 1960, goods traffic continued until 31 January 1966. This picture was taken on 18 August 1967 to accompany the news that it had been purchased by Barnsley Corporation for car parking and for a possible extension to the College of Technology. The station occupied 6.6 acres of land, from the bottom of Regent Street through to Old Mill Street.

There was a time when summer Saturday scenes like this were repeated at stations
all over the country, as factories and mills broke up for their annual holidays. These
are Barnsley Feast holidaymakers in August 1969. The previous year had been the
first time that fare increases were subject to a market-based policy. The cost of a
First Class single between London and Manchester went up from 74s 9d to 90s. At
the same time the London–Sheffield cheap period return fell from 67s to 60s.

Barnsley Station.

Barnsley Station in December 1988.

Barnsley Station was cordoned off in December 1988 when a bomb was discovered in the gents' toilet. An Army bomb disposal unit was called in to deal with the device.

Like most towns, Swinton once boasted more than one railway station. The first to go was Swinton Central which closed on 15 September 1958. Midland Station closed to goods traffic on 4 May 1964 and to passengers on 1 January 1968, although advertised summer Saturday trains continued to call there from 1 June to 7 September of that year.

The new station opened on 16 May 1990 with Councillor Jack Meredith, chairman of the South Yorkshire Passenger Transport Authority, doing the honours and unveiling a plaque to mark the occasion.

LNER 0-6-2T No.3190, pictured here at Doncaster, had originally been built by the Great Northern Railway as the prototype for a new class of tank engines designed to work suburban trains in and out of Kings Cross. However, No.190, as she was then, proved a little too heavy over certain lines necessitating changes in the design of the production engines so as to redistribute the weight.

Designated Class N1 by the GNR a total of 56 of these sturdy machines were built between April 1907 and June 1912. All but four of them were fitted with condensing apparatus which returned exhaust steam back into the water tanks. Almost all the class went new to London, where no fewer than 50 were allocated, and many of these were assigned to working trains over Metropolitan lines. The GNR certainly got their money's worth out of the London-based engines, working them double shifted on routes such as Kings Cross to Alexandra Palace and High Barnet.

Too heavy for this kind of work, No.190 was banished to Yorkshire where, except for a short spell at Hatfield, she spent much of her career. Weighing a little over 64.7 tons in full working order, No.190 carried 4 tons of coal and 1600 gallons of water. Of this, 1100 gallons were held in her side tanks, the remainder in two shallow tanks under the coal space in the bunker. Her condensing apparatus was removed during 1927.

Following the 1923 amalgamation, the LNER added 3000 to the numbers of former GNR locomotives. On nationalisation, the class became Nos.69430–69485 in order. No.3190 received her BR number No.69430 in March 1949, but it was September 1951 before the last of the class got theirs. No.69430 was withdrawn in December 1956, and the class became extinct three years later, on the withdrawal of No.69477 in April 1959. (Collection Clive Hardy)

Designed by Nigel Gresley, the N2s were the first new 0-6-2T design for the GNR since the N1s. The first ten (GNR Nos.1606-1615) were built at Doncaster between December 1920 and April 1921, and as they were required to work over Metropolitan Railway lines, Gresley gave them a very short chimney to keep them within the loading gauge. Another distinguishing feature was the high-pitched boiler.

An order for a further 50 N2s was placed with the North British Locomotive Co of Glasgow in January 1920, and was increased to 60 a couple of months later. Following the amalgamation, the LNER placed orders for N2s with Beyer, Peacock & Co, Manchester; Hawthorn, Leslie & Co; and the Yorkshire Engine Co. Pictured here at Doncaster in October 1949 is No.69551, one of the twelve built by Beyer, Peacock & Co in 1925.

This is former North Eastern Railway Class Y heavy mineral traffic 4-6-2T No.1129 at Doncaster in April 1939. They were designed in 1910 when William Worsdell was Chief Mechanical Engineer of the North Eastern Railway, and were a development of the railway's Class X 4-8-0T shunting engines. Though powerful, these 87.5 ton locomotives carried only 2300 gallons of water and 5 tons of coal, as their work was essentially short-haul between collieries and coal staithes at ports such as West Hartlepool and Stockton. In all, 20 Class Ys were built in one batch at Darlington Works between October 1910 and June 1911. By this time, Worsdell had retired and was succeeded by Vincent Raven.

Under the LNER the engines were designated Class A7, and during the 1930s a number were redeployed to work in marshalling yards. Others worked stone trains, and Nos 1126 and 1175 were diagrammed to haul chalk from a quarry at Hessle on the Humber to a cement works at Stoneferry.

All 20 passed into BR ownership, the class becoming extinct in December 1957 on the withdrawal of BR Nos.69773 (NER No.1129) 69782 (NER No.1182) and 69786 (NER No.1191). (N. Fields)

One of the oldest pictures in the *Star* archives, this shot is of Gresley LNER A4 streamlined express passenger locomotive No.2509 *Silver Link* at Doncaster in March 1936. It's a pity this picture isn't in colour, as the first four engines of this class were turned out in an attractive blue and grey livery.

Once the LNER Board had given the go ahead for the A4 project on 28 March 1935 it took just 186 days to design and build the first one. Though Sir Nigel Gresley was an outstanding engineer, he was never afraid to seek advice and the A4 project was helped along by the National Physics Laboratory and the City & Guilds Engineering College, South Kensington. Gresley also took inspiration for the streamlining from the Bugatti high-speed railcars operating between Paris and Deauville.

Silver Link being prepared for her next turn. BR No.60014 Silver Link was withdrawn in December 1962 but while other A4s withdrawn at the same time – Nos.60003, 60028, 60030 and 60033 – were quickly reduced to piles of scrap, *Silver Link* was not cut up until September the following year.

A4 No.2512 *Silver Fox* at the head of the *Flying Scotsman*.

Preserved LNER A4 No.60009 *Union of South Africa* is one
of the stars of the 1984 BREL Doncaster Works open day.

Henry A Ivatt, the brilliant Crewe-trained engineer, joined the Great Northern in 1895 following the death of Chief Mechanical Engineer Patrick Stirling. Three years later, Doncaster Works turned out No.990, the first of his 4-4-2 express engines. The first locomotive with this wheel arrangement to enter service in the UK, No.990's design featured a large boiler and firebox, resulting in excellent steaming. When these factors were combined with Ivatt's intelligent distribution of her adhesive weight, No.990 was found to be able use her full tractive effort almost immediately, even from a standing start. By 1903, a further 20 of these machines had been built. They were known as 'Klondykes' after the Alaskan gold rush of the day. Behind No.990 is the prototype Class C2 Atlantic No.251. (J.W.Sutherland)

During the 1950s and early 1960s, the Ian Allan Loco Spotters Club organised visits to various locomotive works including Doncaster.

Named after its designer, LNER Class A2/3 Pacific No.500 *Edward Thompson* was the 2000th engine to be completed at the Plant. Thompson had succeeded Sir Nigel Gresley following the latter's untimely death in 1941. Gresley was one of the most dynamic engineers in the history of Britain's railways, and the feeling among many railway enthusiasts and historians is that Thompson resented that fact, spending a lot of time, money and effort in rebuilding perfectly good Gresley engines to test out his theories.

This included rebuilding Gresley's Class P2 2-8-2s, which, despite their unusual wheel arrangement for a British railway, had performed well north of the border on Edinburgh to Aberdeen services since 1934. Thompson rebuilt the P2s into Class A2/2 4-6-2s and sent them back to Scotland, only to have them slated as little better than useless by their crews.

Thompson also had Darlington Works complete the last four Class V2 2-6-2s, then under construction, as what turned out to be underpowered Class A2/1 4-6-2s. However, Thompson was working under wartime conditions when 'make do and mend' was the order of the day, and several of his innovations, such as rocking firegrates and ashpans, were sound. Thompson was succeeded in 1946 by Arthur Peppercorn, and one of Peppercorn's first acts was to cancel the construction of the A2/3s for his own A2 version.

A crowd estimated at 50,000 strong turned up at Doncaster Works in November 1970 to see the renaming of Peppercorn A2 Pacific *Blue Peter* performed by Valerie Singleton of BBC children's TV programme *Blue Peter*.

Blue Peter in action. Later based at the North Yorkshire Moors Railway until its boiler ticket expired in 2002, *Blue Peter* is now at Barrow Hill Roundhouse in need of an overhaul that will cost in excess of £600,000.

Railway enthusiasts from far and wide gathered at Doncaster Works in February 1982 for the 'farewell' open day for BR's English Electric Type 5 Co-Co Class 55 Deltics. Having been replaced on East Coast Main Line services by HST 125 sets there was a proposal to transfer the Deltic fleet to working Newcastle–York–Sheffield–Derby–Birmingham–Bristol trains but it was ruled out due to increasing maintenance costs keeping the Deltics in first class condition. The final nail in the proposal's coffin was hammered home with the arrival of another batch of 125s on the scene.

Enthusiasts make the most of their afternoon. It would be many years before so many Deltics were brought together again in one place again.

Deltic No.55002 *The King's Own Yorkshire Light Infantry* was among the last of the class to be withdrawn from service along with Nos. 55001 *Royal Scots Grey*, 55009 *Alycidon* and 55015 *Tulyar*.

Deltic No.55009 *Alycidon* manoeuvres through the Works.

Deltic No.55009 *Alycidon* is about to cut through the tape, marking its official handing over to the Deltic Preservation Society.

A flashback to what the Deltics were all about; hauling fast passenger expresses along the East Coast Mail Line.

In 1982, Doncaster began construction of the 3300hp Class 58 freight locomotives, the first (No.58001) being completed in the November. The design was born out of the recession-hit early 1980s, when BR found itself in need of a freight locomotive that was relatively inexpensive to build and maintain. The last of the class (No.58050) was completed in 1987. It had been hoped that costs would have been offset by export orders. Alas they never appeared.

Doncaster's first station was built in 1848 as a temporary structure with just two platforms. It was replaced two years later by the station pictured here. During the 1870s and 1880s the Great Northern spent a large amount of money upgrading and enlarging the station, including lengthening existing platforms and adding new ones.

Doncaster Station in the early 1900s.

This is a Doncaster to Sheffield Midland working timetable dating from the late 1960s. Working timetables were issued to operating staff and gave additional information not shown on timetables published for use by the public.

J 10 **WEEKDAYS**		DONCASTER AND SHEFFIELD MIDLAND TO LEEDS AND BRADFORD										
DOWN		1 C69	1N04		1N05	3C73	1M24	1N32		1 C69	1N06	1M22	1N78
			09 15 from Cleethorpes		08 20 from Kings Cross	11 50 E.C.S. from Wakefield C.S.	To Manchester Vic.	07 25 from Bristol		09 25 from Kings Cross	To Liverpool Ex.	09 05 from St. Pancras
		DMU	DMU			DMU	DMU		DMU		DMU	
Timing Load Tons					385 27 D					385 27 D		315 25 D
DONCASTER .. arr	1	..	..		11 06½	..	..	..		11 44	..	..
dep	2	..	..		11 12½	..	..	..		11 47	..	..
Bentley Crossing.. ..	3	..	..		11 16	..	..	..		11 50½	..	..
Carcroft and Adwick	4	..	..		..	..	..	..		..	..	..
Applehurst Jn. ..	5	..	10 48		..	..	..	..		..	..	..
		..	10 55		11 19	..	..	..		11 53½	..	..
Adwick Jn.	6	..	..		..	..	..	..		..	..	..
South Elmsall ..	7	..	11 01½		11 22½	..	..	..		11 57	..	..
SHEFFIELD MID. ..	8	..	..		..	..	..	11 15		..	..	11 59½
Dearne Jn. ..	9	..	..		..	..	..	11 40		..	..	12 21
Moorthorpe ..	10	..	..		..	..	..	11 50		..	..	12 31
South Kirkby Jn. ..	11	..	..		..	..	..	11 53½		..	..	12 34½
Hemsworth ..	12	..	11 07		..	..	..	..			..	..
Fitzwilliam ..	13	..	11 11		..	..	..	..		..	..	..
Hare Park Jn. ..	14	..	11 14½		11 29½	..	12 01			12 07	..	12 42
Crofton West Jn.	15	..	..		..	..	..	..		..	..	..
WAKEFIELD arr	16	..	..		..	..	..	..		..	..	..
KIRKGATE dep	17	..	..		..	..	11 55	..		..	..	..
WAKEFIELD arr	18	..	11 20		11 35	11†58	..	12 06		12 12	..	12 47
WESTGATE .. dep	19	..	11 24		11 38	..	..	12 08		12 15	..	12 50
Ardsley ..	20	..	11 31½ / 11 37½		11 46 / 11 52½	..	1—12 08	12 16½ / 12 23½		12 23 / 12 29½	..	12 58½ / 13 05½
Gelderd Rd. Jn. ..	21	..			..	..					..	
Wortley South Jn. ..	22	..			..	..					..	
Holbeck Jn. ..	23	..			..	To work 12 19 to Huddersfield		1—12 35			..	
Whitehall Jn. ..	24	..			..						..	
LEEDS CITY .. arr	25	..	11 43		11 58			12 29		12 35	..	13 11
dep	26	11 35	..		..		12†06	..		12†36	12 43	13 05	13 21
Leeds City Parcels Depot..	27	..	..		..		..	..		..	..	..
Whitehall Jn. ..	28	11 38	..		..		12 09	..		12 39	12 46	13 08
Holbeck Jn. ..	29	11 39	..		..		12 10	..		12 40	12 47	13 09
Wortley West Jn. ..	30	..	..		..		..	..		..	..	..
Stanningley ..	31	11 46	..		..		12 17	..		12 47	..	13 16
New Pudsey.. arr	32	..	..		..		..	..		12 57	..	
dep	33	..	..		..		..	..		12 59	..	
LAISTERDYKE ..	34	11 50½	..		..		12 21½	..		12 51½	13 02½	13 20½
Bowling Jn. ..	35	..	..		..		..	..		..	..	
Low Moor ..	36	..	..		..		..	..		..	..	
Hammerton St. Depot ..	37	..	..		..		..	..		..	..	
BRADFORD EX. arr	38	11 56	..		..		12 27	..		12 57	13 09	13 26

Thousands turned up at Doncaster in July 1988 to watch the celebrations marking the 50th anniversary of Gresley Pacific *Mallard* taking the world speed record for steam traction.

Between 1987 and 1988 British Rail passenger numbers had risen by 8 per cent to 20.6 billion passenger miles, the highest for 27 years. Total receipts were up by 13 per cent at 1.622 million, and the Group as a whole generated a surplus of £291 million including property sales. Prime Minister Margaret Thatcher never hid her dislike of British Rail, yet despite the anti-rail rhetoric and the slashing of Government support, the company not only turned in an operating surplus of £107 million – £304 million when property sales were taken into account – it also proved to be the most cost-effective railway in Europe at the time.

In the Cabinet reshuffle of 26 July, pro-rail Sir David Mitchell was replaced by Michael Portillo, and by October the press was reporting that the Government was considering selling off parts of the network to regional companies. Warnings that privatisation would wreck any chance of an integrated transport policy fell on deaf ears. That it would also break up a near self-sufficient industry into any number disparate entities did not seem to matter.

However, one early proposal for privatisation was for British Rail to remain intact, responsible of track, signalling, stations, rolling stock, and maintaining services deemed to be of social necessity. Private operators could bid to operate certain services such as all East Coast Main Line expresses between London–Edinburgh–Aberdeen for which they would pay a premium; the operative word being pay, and not subsidise. Similarly companies could bid to operate freight services, meaning that the National Coal Board would have been able to run its own merry-go-round coal trains to power stations.

InterCity liveried 89001 at Doncaster.

On 26 April 1994, the first ever 6E56 Tunstead–Drax desulphurisation train, hauled by National Power owned Class 59 No.59201 *Vale of York*, pauses at Doncaster for a crew change. (Baz Blood)

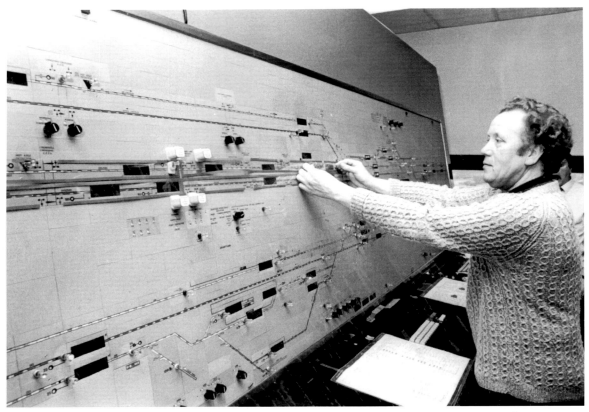

The resignalling and electrification of the East Coast Main Line was a protracted affair thanks mainly to Government red tape, with outline approval for work as far north as Doncaster being granted in 1972. A new signalling centre was to be built at Doncaster replacing no less than 51 mechanical boxes and covering 155 route miles, and the new signalling equipment was to be compatible with an electrified line. When first planned, the resignalling would have cost £25 million, but thanks to the delays it cost £40 million.

The aftermath of a collision between a diesel multiple unit and a lorry on Alexander Street level crossing, Thorne, near Doncaster in July 1969.

ON SHED

As land was never a problem at Millhouses, the Midland were able to lay out the depot so that facilities were used to maximum efficiency. Here 'Baby Scot' 4-6-0 No.5905 *Lord Rathmore* stands alongside the coaling stage on 9 July 1933. This class came about following the successful introduction into traffic of the three-cylinder Royal Scot Class on West Coast Anglo-Scottish expresses.

The older four-cylinder Claughton Class 4-6-0s, though capable of fast running, were heavy on coal and even heavier on repair bills. Derby Works came up with the idea of sticking a Claughton boiler on top of a three-cylinder chassis based on the Royal Scot design, with the result that Claughtons Nos.5902 and 5971 were taken in hand for conversion.

They turned out to be not so much rebuilds as brand new engines. All that remained of the original engines were the wheel centres, bogies and a few odds and sods. Nos.5902 and 5971 were an instant success, and a further 40 'rebuilds' were authorised. No.5905 was rebuilt at Derby in 1933 and later renumbered No.5533. (C.M & J.M. Bentley)

Situated between Heeley Station and Millhouses & Ecclesall Station, Millhouses engine shed was opened by the Midland Railway in 1901 as its main depot for passenger engines in the Sheffield area. Pictured on shed is domeless boilered Stanier Jubilee Class 4-6-0 No.5607 on 15 September 1935. The engine was about one year old and had yet to receive its name – *Fiji*. (C.M.& J.M. Bentley)

Former 'crimson ramblers' Nos.41016 and 41030 at Millhouses shed on 3 April 1949. No.41016 was a local engine and remained allocated to Millhouses until its withdrawal from service in October 1951. No.41030 had come from Bristol from where it was withdrawn in August 1951. Sheffield's last compound, No.40907, left for Doncaster under its own steam in September 1960. (L.W. Good courtesy of the Gordon Coltas Photographic Trust)

There had been a locomotive depot of one sort or another at Grimesthorpe (Brightside) since the 1860s, when the Midland constructed one of its classic true roundhouses, with lines radiating out from a turntable inside a circular building. With the opening of the Sheffield to Chesterfield line in 1870 it soon became apparent that the company would have to increase its engine servicing facilities, and a new shed with a 46ft turntable was built slightly to the north of the existing one.

Further expansion took place during the late 1890s when an eight-road fitting shop was added. Space and expensive trackwork were avoided with the installation of a traverser. During 1901 a new 60ft turntable with lines radiating from it was added outdoors, enabling the 1860s building to be taken out of use. Pictured at Grimesthorpe on 1 May 1930 is Hughes/Fowler 2-6-0 No.13138. (C.M. & J.M. Bentley)

Darnall was originally planned by the LNER to be a depot for its Manchester–Sheffield electric locomotives, but due to the war, work on the four-road electric shed had to be abandoned in 1940. From 1943 Darnall serviced steam locomotives instead. The ten-road steam shed could accommodate up to 70 engines, and the depot's 70ft turntable could handle the largest LNER locomotives likely to use it. The electric shed was completed in 1952 but served this function for just 8 years, after which it was used for diesel locos. Our picture – taken on 9 September 1959 – shows the electric shed occupied by diesel multiple units (DMUs).

DMUs were developed primarily for working local and branch line services in order to reduce operating costs. In late 1952 the Government approved a £1.5 million investment programme for two-car DMUs. Designed and built by Derby Carriage & Wagon Works, the DMUs were of light alloy construction; each car powered by two Leyland six-cylinder horizontal-type 125hp engines. Although passenger seating was of the bus type, the design of the cars afforded good views nonetheless. Two two-car units could be coupled together and operated in multiple by a single driver. There were many designs over the years.

Shedman Keith Fieldhouse who had been given the task of keeping the floor at Darnall Diesel Maintenance Depot free of grease and oil, demonstrates the automatic floor cleaner. The cleaner sprayed detergent on the floor, scrubbed up the dirt and then sucked up the surplus water.

On 24 June 1964, BR invited *Sheffield Star* journalists and photographers to have a look round the new maintenance depot at Tinsley. Six tracks entered the depot from either end but did not run all the way through, as the central area was taken up with the machine shop and stores. The depot could hold 24 main line locomotives at a time under cover, and Tinsley's fitters were able deal with up to ten per shift. Once on line Tinsley Traction Maintenance Depot became the maintenance facility for all diesel locomotives allocated to the Sheffield area. (British Railways Eastern Region)

This picture taken at Tinsley clearly shows how the layout of the facility enabled fitters to work on any part of a locomotive. Despite it being a state-of-the-art maintenance depot it was not equipped to undertake power unit changes, hence the lack of overhead cranes. (British Railways Eastern Region)

The diesel locomotive servicing facility at Tinsley Yard. (British Railways Eastern Region)

The Hawker-Siddeley/Sulzer Kestrel project was a private venture, although BR had some input into the design as, at the time, the Eastern Region was considering acquiring 100mph 4000hp super Deltics. Work commenced on the locomotive in 1965 at the Brush Works, Loughborough, while the 16-cylinder Sulzer 16LVA24 power unit was built in France.

Officially designated the HS4000, the locomotive had an overall length of 66ft 6in and semi-streamlined cab fronts fitted with Triplex wrap-round windscreens. The power unit was capable of a continuous top speed of 100mph; a maximum service speed of 125mph, and a design top speed of 130mph. A lot of thought also went into the internal layout so as to reduce maintenance time and costs. Though nominally allocated to Tinsley, from 14 May 1968 Kestrel was outbased at Shirebrook where it took part in trials on duties normally assigned to Class 47 diesel-electrics.

The following August Kestrel took part in a heavy-haul trial. She took a 2028-ton train from Mansfield to Lincoln; a route which included a standing start on a 1 in 150 rising gradient in wet weather. Towards the end of the year, the locomotive was fitted with Class 47 bogies so that it could be trialled on passenger services, and in mid-June 1969 it took over a Deltic diagram. When it came to heavy-haul Kestrel was about 15 years ahead of its time. The locomotive was sold to the USSR in 1971.

Preserved Stanier Black
Five 4-6-0 No.44932 at
a Tinsley open day.

Tinsley's capacity was 190 main line and 80 shunting locomotives. On a number of occasions Sheffield Parkway
played host to locomotives running away from the depot. This ensemble piece, which did a runner during 1978,
gained sufficient momentum to push shunt engine 08223 almost onto the carriageway itself.

" 'Ello, 'ello 'ello. What's all this then?" On 19 December 1978 several of Sheffield's finest were confronted with an unusual parking problem caused by Class 56 No.56003 doing a runner.

A few months later and it was the turn of this pair of Class 20s.

Built by the Yorkshire Engine Co of Sheffield in 1959, this Janus Class 0-6-0 diesel-electric shunter was originally used by the National Coal Board at Littleton Colliery, Cannock. It is seen here in 2008 on shed at the Churnet Valley Railway's shed, with Cheddleton buffered up to preserved Gresley V2 No.4771 *Green Arrow*. The diesel had previously been with the Ribble Steam Railway, Preston Docks, and when this picture was taken was still sporting its Ribble Rail blue livery. (Clive Hardy)

204hp 0-6-0 diesel shunter D2229 was built for BR by Vulcan Foundry, Newton-le-Willows in 1955 but after only 15 years service it was sold to the National Coal Board for use at NCB Brookhouse Colliery, Beighton. After a few months it was transferred to NCB Orgreave Colliery, but was back at Brookhouse by the end of March 1972. Further service at Orgreave followed during 1973, with D2229 returning to Brookhouse in 1974 where it remained until moving to NCB Manton Colliery in March 1983. On 26 May 1990 the engine arrived at the South Yorkshire Railway Preservation Society's site at Meadowhall and remained there until 2002 when the society decamped to Peak Rail. (Clive Hardy)

27000 in retirement at the Midland Railway Centre, Butterley, Derbyshire, in 2006. In 1989, whilst running as NS No.1502, she took part in the 150th anniversary celebrations of the building of the first railway in the Netherlands. (Clive Hardy)

For the best part of 30 years, railway enthusiasts travelling south along the Tinsley Viaduct of the M1, if they looked left, would have observed a couple of saddletanks in the yard of Harrison & Sons (Transport) Ltd. In October 2005 they suddenly disappeared, re-emerging at the Ecclesbourne Railway in Wirksworth, Derbyshire.

Both are pictured here on 15 August 2006. No.3 was built by the firm of Andrew Barclay & Co of Kilmarnock in 1954; the other one, looking somewhat grubby but in fact protected with a layer of grease and oil, was also built by Barclays, but

in 1947. At the time these pictures were taken, No.3 had been moved to a more accessible location at Wirksworth to be assessed for returning to steam. Though underpowered for working the line from Wirksworth to Duffield, these engines would be ideal for use on the branch line to the quarry. (Clive Hardy)

A new arrival at Sheffield Transport Museum in August 1985 was this Austerity 0-6-0ST.

"And now for something completely different." Stage Director Robin Burch stands proudly on the front of the full-size locomotive that he and his staff made for a forthcoming production of *The Railway Children* at Sheffield's Crucible Theatre in September 1984.

Publicity call for the Crucible Theatre's production of *The Railway Children*.

THE SOUTH YORKSHIRE
SUPERTRAM

Not everyone was keen to see Sheffield acquire a new tramway system. When the project first received the go-ahead, it was understood that all costs would be met with a straightforward financing arrangement through the Department of Transport. As usual, politics got in the way and agreements were broken. The Supertram project eventually cost in excess of £240 million, of which £66.6 million was covered by a Section 56 grant from the Department of Transport and £13.1 million from the EU. The remainder was covered by non-trading and trading borrowing arrangements and developed contributions, some of which would be recovered with the sale of the operating franchise.

The launch of the Supertram project in December 1990 included this mock-up of how the new vehicles might look. In 1976, just 16 years after Sheffield had gained its place in British transport history as the last major city in England to scrap its tramway, a new study recommended their reintroduction.

Construction work underway along the High Street. We have included the Supertram in this railway book because it is more akin to a light railway than to the street tramway system once operated. Trams stop at stations and there is a sophisticated signalling and control system in operation. Also the Supertram comes within the jurisdiction of the Railways Inspectorate.

The view up Commercial Street to High Street.

The impressive way the tram tracks sweep and climb in certain areas of the city was captured in this image taken from the Norfolk Park area by Ron Lane on 23 June 1994.

The first unit arrives from the manufacturers.

Almost a driver's eye view. The cabs at each end are identical, and are segregated from the passengers for driver safety and comfort. Drivers are aided by onboard computer systems that monitor equipment, and in the event of a fault can run a diagnostic and display information on a panel in the cab. As with the electric locomotives that once operated between Sheffield Victoria and Manchester, these trams are equipped with regenerative braking systems. Whenever the driver applies the brakes, the tram's eight traction motors act as dynamos and generate electricity, which is returned to the overhead power supply.

The initial order for 25 double articulated trams was placed with the German firm of Siemens/Dueway. At the time of their completion these trams were among the largest of their type in Europe, having an overall length of almost 35 metres and weighing 52 tonnes. The carrying capacity in excellent each unit has seating for 88 and standing room for 162.

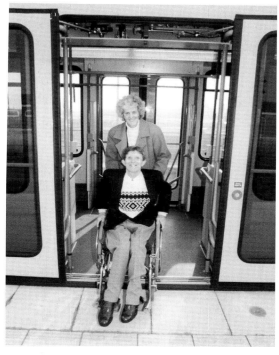

There are a number of reasons why the trams have low floor entrances. Firstly, it was decided that tram station platforms would themselves be at a low level. More important, however, was having vehicles that allowed ease of access for physically impaired passengers, wheelchair users and children's buggies.

On 17 September 1993 the Supertram was out on a trial run between its depot and Meadowhall.

Part of the system runs over ballasted railway track, while the 750V DC overhead conductor wires are positioned at either 5m or 6.3m above the railhead. The wires are supported by cantilevers attached to poles. More modern systems such as the tramway that began operating in Nice in November 2007 do not have overhead wires in areas that are environmentally sensitive. The trams stop, lower their pantographs and then proceed through the area on battery power. Once clear they stop, raise their pantographs and set off once more.

A temporary terminus for the trams in Fitzalan Square in February 1995. On 22 August 1994, the second stage (Fitzalan Square to Spring Lane) was opened, followed by Spring Lane to Gleadless Town on 5 December 1994. Where trams, pedestrians and road vehicles share the right of way, SE1-35G grooved rail is used.

The tramway infrastructure in the High Street area of
the city centre was complete by mid-February 1995.

Supertram and traffic at Woodbourn Road in March 1994.

Though the system opened in stages, these did not follow the order in which they were constructed. The line between Fitzalan Square and Meadowhall was the first to go live on 21 March 1994, and two days later it was officially opened by HRH the Princess Royal.

It is 16 February 1995 and for the first time a tram makes a nighttime test run through the heart of the city. The test was carried out at walking pace to ensure the safety of the tram, pedestrians and motorists.

The junctions of Haymarket, Commercial Street and High Street from Fitzalan Square on 18 March 1995.

There are times, such as during heavy snowfalls, when the Supertram comes into its own, continuing to operate normally while road traffic crawls along.

Supertram passengers take advantage of free rides on 23 October 1995 in celebration of the opening of the final section between Hillsborough and Middlewood.

At Heart Ltd Titles

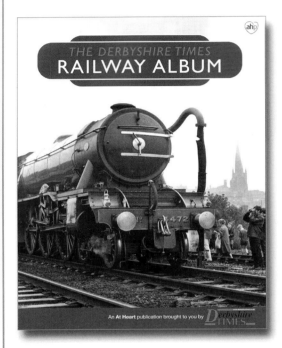

The Derbyshire Times Railway Album
£14.99
ISBN: 978-1-84547-200-9

The Derbyshire Times Railway Album gives readers a closer look around Derbyshire's most distinctive trains and railways through a stunning selection of photographs from throughout the 20th century.

Packed full of fascinating facts about the region's most renowned routes – the Cromford & High Peak line, the old Midland main from Derby to Manchester, and through the Hope Valley, to name but a few – *The Derbyshire Times Railway Album* promises to be an essential companion for the railway enthusiast and general reader alike.

If you would like any further information on the above title please contact us at the address below.
At Heart Ltd: 32 Stamford Street, Altrincham, Cheshire, WA14 1EY **Tel:** 0161 924 0159 **Fax:** 0161 924 0160